Danielle Gauss,
Internationally Board Certified

The Booby Fairy's Guide
to Breastfeeding

Second Edition

Foreword By Cerina Vincent

ISBN: 9798390649732 (paperback)

This book is the work of nonfiction. Names and identifying characteristics have been changed to protect their identities. Written permission received for each photograph.

Disclaimer: The advice contained in this book may not be suitable for every situation, and should not replace receiving professional services and medical advice from licensed practitioners. Readers should be aware that internet websites listed in this book may have changed or disappeared between when this work was written to when it is read.

Front Cover Image Dr.Michelle Weaver, DC
Cover Design by Danielle Gauss
Author website: www.daniellegauss.com

Video Class series available for purchase at the above site.

ABOUT THE AUTHOR

Danielle Gauss, IBCLC, is an advanced-practice Internationally Board Certified Lactation Consultant based out of Orange County, California. She is trained in oral tethering, specializing in the identification and treatment of lip ties, tongue ties, and buccal and posterior tethering. She specializes in proper bodywork following frenectomy, including the importance of acupressure calming points and craniosacral therapy. She received her education from the University of California San Diego. Danielle obtained her board certification as a lactation consultant through the International Board of Lactation Examiners. Over the course of her twenty year career, she has assisted in numerous births and helped educate thousands of women about the birth process and the breastfeeding needs of their infants. She had the unique opportunity to work as an IBCLC both in a hospital setting for four years and in a pediatric office for nine years before settling into her new home base in Orange County five years ago. Danielle has been married for twenty-two years and is the mother of two beautiful grown women.

Danielle Gauss, IBCLC
www.daniellegauss.com

Instagram: @daniellegaussibclc @tonguetietribe
TikTok: @theboobyfairy

I would like to dedicate this book to my two beautiful daughters, Alyssa and Alaina. Without them, I would have never gained the insight needed to pursue my passion for helping women and their babies.

Foreword

I've always thought of myself as a "natural" person. I've always gotten weird reactions to prescription medications and bizarre hives and rashes from fake ingredients. When I was fifteen, I was eating gluten-free (back when they called it "wheat-free") and planned to a homeopathic doctor. I was reading ingredients on labels long before it was trendy and cool.

Now, I had my share of years addicted to Diet Red Bull. And I used to eat way too many processed protein bars and artificially sweetened frozen yogurt full of chemicals. But now, for the most part, I enjoy real food and try to make healthy, natural choices.

I'm also an actor and writer and have been in the entertainment business for over twenty-five years. I've found that focusing on what I put *into my body* always gives me more energy and makes me feel more confident in my wardrobe on TV, movie sets, and the red carpet. I co-wrote a book on this stuff in my twenties called *How to Eat Like a Hot Chick*. Eating healthy and balanced really was/is my passion.

So when I got pregnant at thirty-nine years old (insert geriatric pregnancy joke here), I knew without a question *I was going to breastfeed!* No way I was going to give my baby processed powdered stuff they make in a lab that would make me itchy and ill if I drank it. There was no other option for me. I was going to breastfeed—no matter what.

Once I announced my pregnancy on social media, I got a DM on my Instagram. It was Danielle Gauss, whom I'd gone to high school with. We were in theatre together, and her mother was my

2

drama teacher. We hadn't spoken in twenty years, but as soon as Danielle saw that I was pregnant, she reached out to me and said,

"Hey, girl, congrats! Just wanted to reach out and let you know that I'm the lead lactation consultant for a big pediatric practice in LA and Orange County. Also have many celebrity clients. Let me know if you have any questions or need help feeding when your little one arrives, free of charge. You will be a fantastic momma! Also, I have a lot of info on my website.

I was so moved. We all know as soon as you're pregnant *everyone* has an opinion and *everyone* thinks they are an expert. But here was an old pal from high school offering *her help*. For free. And she *is* an expert. I thought it was very kind.

But then, I thought, *I'll be fine. I won't need any help.*

HA! Oh, Mama, was I wrong. I'll spare you the gory details of my attempt at a natural birth at a birth center that turned into a very scary emergency C-section at a hospital. It was all the things I didn't want for my baby and myself.

After my C-section drama, I was hanging on to my last wish.

I WILL breastfeed. Do not give my baby formula. I will nurse him exclusively. I know I can do it.

And, wow, was I humbled. Learning how to breastfeed while recovering from C-section surgery, vomiting from the pain meds, and being beyond sleep deprived is *insane*. The lactation nurses in the hospital are *angels*. And so is Danielle. Actually, Danielle's a fairy. A Booby Fairy.☺ When my son's birth was announced in *People*, I got another DM:

"Hey, friend. If you are choosing to breastfeed and struggle at all, just say the word, and I'll come help. It's not supposed to hurt, so if it does, something needs to be adjusted. Here is my number. Feel free to text with questions."

I saw it—but I didn't even respond. I was so deep into those gnarly first weeks of motherhood, I didn't have the energy to even type "thank you" or send a simple "heart" emoji.

But I knew I needed help, so I hired a random lactation lady to come to my house. I didn't want to bother my old friend from high school. Honestly, I was embarrassed. I felt like I was failing, so I'd rather a stranger see me fail than some beautiful, successful expert mother I went to high school with. So I spent too much money on a lactation nurse to come to my house. She looked at my son, said his mouth looked "fine," showed me how to latch properly, and said I was doing a good job.

But something wasn't right. My milk came in, I was engorged, I was nursing literally around the clock, but my baby was screaming and starving and not gaining weight. One night at 3 a.m., the first time in days I'd had more than one hour of sleep, I was awoken by the most excruciating pain. My boobs were the size of watermelons and hard as rocks, and it was impossible for my son to get his tiny mouth on to latch. He was screaming and starving. I was screaming in pain. I felt like I had a thousand razor blades shooting through my boobs. We desperately tried to put the breast pump together. I had red lines crawling up the basketballs under my skin towards my neck. I had chills. I had a fever. Yep, I had *mastitis.*

I got a round of antibiotics from my amazing midwife, who told me to stop nursing, to just give my son formula, take the pressure off, and enjoy my baby. Plus, he wasn't gaining weight and he needed it. My pediatrician said the same thing.

That's not what I wanted to hear. I *wanted* to breastfeed! So, I paid for another lactation consultant and ordered a hospital grade breast pump. Now I was pumping *and* nursing around the clock, desperately trying to keep up my milk supply, feed my baby, and get the milk out of my body so I wouldn't get mastitis again. Even though I was nursing constantly, he was still not gaining weight! He was eating and pooping, but not gaining pounds. We did that for a couple more weeks, then…BAM! I got mastitis again.

Back to another lactation consultant and my pediatrician, both of whom looked in his mouth and said he was fine. But since he was still not gaining weight, I was now ordered to start him on formula.

So I stood with a fever and chills in a Whole Foods, reading the labels on dozens of brands of baby formula and sobbing. I was so upset. And I didn't want the formula to mess with my milk supply! I knew I had milk—so why wasn't he gaining weight? I was dumbfounded and confused.

Exhausted and engorged, I posted a photo in the middle of the night of my skinny little baby trying to nurse, with a message talking about my mastitis.

I got another DM from the Booby Fairy. She told me exactly what to do: soak my boobs in Epsom salt and rub out the clogs with a vibrator or electric toothbrush. She told me what homeopathic meds and herbs to take and what oils to rub on my boobs that were safe for my baby. She sent me a mile-long message with exact instructions that literally SAVED me. Then she offered her support once again.

And this time I put my ego and insecurities aside and took her help. When I walked into her office, she gave me a warm hug and got right to work. She took my sweet boy into her arms and handled him in a way that I didn't know a baby could be handled. She soothed him in an instant. And before she'd even examined him, she kindly said,

"You're not doing anything wrong. Your sweet baby has a tongue-tie."

"No, he doesn't!" I cried! "Everyone has looked in his mouth! His pediatrician, my midwife, four lactation consultants, everyone!"

Danielle politely and professionally replied,

"I'm 100% certain he has tongue and mouth ties. Your baby is working so hard to eat—it's like sucking a thick milkshake through a tiny straw with a hole on it, all while on a treadmill! He's burning so many calories trying to eat, he can't gain weight. That's why he's peeping and pooping but also why you're getting sick. He can't get the milk out sufficiently or completely."

"But I'm pumping AND giving him bottles of formula!" I cried. Literally. I was crying. Like ugly-crying.

She explained that he couldn't eat well from the bottle, either, but that if I followed her instructions, my baby would start gaining weight, sleep better, and be happier. You'd think I would have run to get his tongue tie fixed, right?

Ha! Nope. I didn't. I was scared. His dad thought it was a fad. I was filming a movie. I was tired and overwhelmed. So, I suffered longer. And so did our baby. I was three months in, and he still wasn't gaining weight properly. I posted a photo of him on IG and got another DM from Danielle.

"I can tell he has ties by his little face. Please get a consult. It will change your life."

I finally listened. And guess what? YEP! Danielle was right.

I did *everything* she said. The pediatric surgeon said he had tongue, mouth, *and* lip ties. They were submucosal, something that most pediatricians are not trained to see.

We fixed his ties and in ten days my child looked like a different baby. He was chunky and fat and squishy and, most important, healthy and happy. He gained wight SO fast! I was still giving him the crappy formula because I had to—but I also never stopped nursing him so he was also getting my antibodies and all the magical things in breastmilk that our bodies make just for our baby.

He's turning three next week—and yes, *I am still nursing him.* All thanks to Danielle. The emotional benefits of nursing into toddlerhood have been amazing! And there's no way he and I would have had this joyful experience if it weren't for the Booby Fairy.

Every mama will have their own breastfeeding journey. And I hope and pray that it's effortless and magical! But if it's not, know that if you are reading this book, you are doing *everything* you can to set you and your baby up for success! Danielle's book is your roadmap through this messy, sticky, milky, tear-filled, painful, joyful, serotonin-boosting adventure with your body and your baby.

7

Danielle saved my milk supply, and honestly, she saved my child and my sanity. She turned a really crappy start into a joyful, blissful, successful breastfeeding journey. I'm so happy that every mama out there gets to have Danielle's wisdom, expertise, and soothing words of encouragement in their hands.

Lots of love and light… and lots and lots of milk! (Unless you have an oversupply, in which case, I'm sure the Booby Fairy has advice for you, too)

XO, Cerina Vincent
–Actor, Author of *Everybody Has a Belly Button*, host of the parenting podcast *Raising Amazing,* and most important, *mother!*

Chapter 1: Breastfeeding: The Why, the What, and the Who

It is 3 a.m. There you lie on your bed, staring at the ceiling, with ice diapers adorning your breasts and nether regions, all while trying to wrap your head around the idea that you just brought a tiny, crying, pooping, life-changing human into the world. Congrats! You officially made it through pregnancy and birth and have entered into the overwhelming life that is parenting. Most likely you have attended many classes, read books, listened to podcasts, and of course googled everything in preparation for this moment. You survived the birth…the rest should be easy right? RIGHT?! Take a breath, Momma, we are just getting started. I've got you, girl! I have been there, and you are not alone.

I will never forget the first time I held my daughter Alyssa in my arms. She was crying, bright eyed, and rooting like crazy. The nurse placed her on my chest, and she began the adorable head bobble that newborns do looking for their first meal. It amazed me just how instinctual everything was.

I didn't understand until that moment how you could completely fall in love with someone you had just met. I was not prepared in the least, but had no other choice but to dive in completely. As terrified as I was, my maternal instincts kicked in, and I knew I would do whatever it took to protect my child. It did not matter what anyone said or did, she was mine, and I would sacrifice my own needs for hers. That is motherhood.

Since the moment you saw the double pink line on your pee stick stating that you were pregnant, I'm sure people have been saying, "You're going to breastfeed, right?" There is a lot of pressure nowadays to breastfeed, and you may feel that if you don't breastfeed you will be classified into a group of "those feeders." Yet you may be thinking, "I think so…I mean, I'll try it…but what about all the horror stories I hear? What about the women who say they had infections and sore nipples and that it was the hardest thing they'd ever done. Is it really worth all that? What if I don't really want to? Will I be looked down upon?"

These are questions that only you can answer, but I would like to ease a little bit of that anxiety if I can.

I remember thinking the first time I latched Alyssa, "What is the big deal? I have breasts, she has a mouth, it is 'natural.' What is the problem?" I didn't understand why everyone was so worked up about it. I was twenty-two and *very* naive. I had my moments, like lying in bed engorged, crying at a Taco Bell commercial because I couldn't decide if I wanted a taco or a mexi-melt. You know, legit baby blues concerns. Postpartum is a hoot, but for the most part,

Alyssa was cake to feed. I had gobs of milk and no issues latching, and I breastfed her till she was nine months old. I thought that this was the greatest, easiest thing ever! But twenty-one months later, Alaina was born. Feeding her, birthing her, and raising her was a completely different ball game. IT…WAS…HARD! I hated it. I will never forget staring at her when she was six days old and thinking, I can't feed her. My nipples are bleeding and possibly will fall off if I latch this baby one more time. My experience with her was completely different.

I was working in the mother/baby unit of the hospital I delivered her in, and I am pretty sure that everyone I worked with saw my nipples. I could not figure out for the life of me why this was so painful, so different. It was the same set of boobs as before, yet there I sat in the middle of the night staring at this tiny 5-pound 12-ounce barracuda baby. It was absolute hell. My professor from UCSD, where I had obtained my training for childbirth education and eventually would do my IBCLC (Internationally Board Certified Lactation Consultant) training, just happened to be in the hospital that day and decided to come see me. First thing she says is, "Oh my goodness, your baby has a heart-shaped tongue!" At the time, I had no clue what that meant, and to be honest, I don't think she did yet either. We knew it was some form of an oral tie, but seventeen years ago we were just starting to pay attention to oral restrictions. (Don't worry, ladies, I have a whole section on tongue ties in this book. Oral ties also known as TOTs or tethered oral tissue, is where the frenulum restricts the function of the tongue, lip, and anatomy of the mouth.) All I knew was that this baby fed differently than my last, and I was miserable.

Everything that could go wrong with breastfeeding went wrong. I had low supply, clogs, mastitis, thrush, and a constantly crying baby with feeding aversions. You name it, I had it. My postpartum depression was through the roof, and I felt extremely alone. There was so much pressure on me to breastfeed because of my job, and I felt trapped. I ended up being a closet bottle feeder, too embarrassed to admit that I wasn't actually putting this baby at the breast. I would pump and bottle-feed her my milk instead (which, by the way, is still breastfeeding) because putting her on the breast was just too hard. I was anxious, paranoid she was starving, worried that she was spitting up constantly, and frustrated that I couldn't provide nourishment to this child like I could with my last baby. I was crying, she was crying, it was a mess. Finally a very wise friend of mine, who also happened to be my OB/GYN, sat me down and gave me permission to quit breastfeeding at five months in. She told me that the most important thing I could do is make sure I fed my baby in a way that makes me the best mom. I needed that permission to quit, and for someone to tell me that I wasn't a horrible mother for changing to formula. Mom guilt is real, you guys. She was absolutely right. My philosophy has always been this:

14

Number 1 : You feed your baby in any way that works.

Number 2: You do what is going to make you the best mom for your baby. That is what is most important.

From that moment on, I knew what I needed to do with my life. I needed to become a lactation consultant to help other mothers going through the challenges that I had. Alaina changed my life path, and I am so very grateful that she did. Sometimes moms need permission from a professional to quit and do what is best for them. I have always made it my goal as an IBCLC to meet moms where they are and help them meet the goals they desire. It has nothing to do with me or my beliefs; it has everything to do with this mother and her baby.

Breastfeeding is not for everyone, and those of us in the lactation consultant/breastfeeding specialists community completely understand that! For some women, the thought of it really makes them uncomfortable, and those mommies may decide to pump and bottle feed only. Which, again, is still breastfeeding. I give a lot of credit to women who make that decision, for that takes strong determination and just shows what an awesome mom they are. Others might want to try and see where it goes. Whatever direction you choose to go, what is important is that you make the choice that is going to make you the best mommy. Remember that every day of breastfeeding is a gift to that baby, whether that be one day or two years. It will provide them with ultimate nutrients and a wonderful start to life.

Overwhelming scientific evidence has proved that breast milk is the most complete form of nutrition for infants. Breast milk is comprised of water, fats, proteins, carbohydrates, minerals, vitamins, DHA/ARA, enzymes, anti-parasitics, anti-allergens, anti-virals, growth hormones, live antibodies, and so much more. There is nothing like it. It is a living fluid with the ability to change based on the needs of the baby and the length of lactation. When the baby latches, his saliva absorbs into the breast, signaling to the mother's body what the baby needs. For example, if your baby is fighting a virus or bacteria, the mother's body will react to the virus in the baby's saliva and create leukocytes and antibodies specific to that illness and pass those antibodies through the milk to the baby. When this happens, you can often see the color of the breastmilk change. The milk will have more of a yellow tinge, which is proof of those cells working.

One of the coolest aspects about breast milk in my opinion is that our bodies can decipher the difference in enzymes and tweak the consistency to match the baby's nutritional needs. If the baby is dehydrated, the mother's body will pour more fluid into the milk for hydration. If the baby needs more fat and protein, then your milk will produce that. It is the perfect food for their gut. The longer a woman lactates, the more she will see the changes in her milk, both in consistency and color. Breast milk can be blue, green, red, yellow, white, and so on. Often, what you eat can also flavor and color the milk. If you have spinach or kale, it will be blueish, and beets can turn it red. Pretty cool, right?

Breasts are sensitive, miracle-giving, superpower love jugs. I'm talking about magnificent slayer-of-viruses-and-diseases and make-a-baby-grow creations. Treat them with respect, people! I have been saying for months that I am sure breast milk could cure Covid. I mean, seriously, has the CDC considered putting breast milk on the coronavirus? I am telling you, women could save this pandemic by making it rain! I can see it now, lactating women standing on balconies, spraying their breastmilk over the streets. We will save humanity! Could you imagine that scene? The speech from Dr. Fauci would be epic.

Breastfeeding reaps great health benefits for not only the baby but the mother, her family, the health care system, and our society as well. Breast milk has been proven to treat conjunctivitis in the eye, skin disorders such as eczema and psoriasis, and ear infections, and it might even prove useful in treating prostate cancer. A scientist who was studying prostate cancer cells in a lab was pumping and accidentally spilled her pumped milk on the petri dish. To her excited surprise, the live components of the milk completely obliterated the cancer. How amazing is that! That has opened up a new realm of cancer research, and you can better believe that if my husband gets prostate cancer, he will absolutely be getting breast milk. I will most likely have to induce lactation on myself, but that is a topic for another chapter.

So let us look at the scientific facts. The American Academy of Pediatrics and the U.S. Surgeon General recommend exclusive breastfeeding for at least the first six months of life to a year, or for however long is desired by mother and baby. The reasons include those we have discussed, as well as others:

Benefits for Baby:
- Breast milk is perfect nutrition that continually changes to meet growth and developmental needs
- Breast milk is easy to digest, resulting in fewer digestive problems
- Antibodies in breast milk keep babies healthier, resulting in fewer ear, respiratory, and urinary tract infections
- Breastfed infants have a decreased incidence of SIDS (Sudden Infant Death Syndrome)
- Breastfed children are less likely to suffer from diabetes, asthma, allergies, obesity, and childhood cancers

Benefits for Mom:
- Helps Mom recover and the uterus to return to prepregnancy size more quickly. In some women, the calorie burn of lactating can also aid in weight loss

- Decreases her risk for type 2 diabetes
- Decreases her risk of breast and ovarian cancer
- Breast milk is always ready to use, easy to transport and access
- Statistically, breastfeeding moms average more sleep than formula-feeding moms.

Some may argue that breastfeeding can even have societal benefits by saving on long-term health care, being kinder to the environment, and resulting in fewer missed days of work for the mother. So, yes, there is overwhelming scientific evidence that breastmilk is better than formula. However, I never want a woman to feel ashamed for how she chooses to feed her baby, period.

Ultimately, breastfeeding is a mother's choice. You have to do what is best for you and your baby, but also what is going to make you a better mother in the long run. If this is your first time breastfeeding, be sure to surround yourself with women who support you. It takes a village. Seriously, back in the day, a village of aunties would pass babies along and breastfeed each other's kids. They supported and lifted each other up. This is what we need to do as women. Breastfeeding is hard. Parenting is hard. Being a woman is hard. We have to learn as a society to lift each other up in a way that is loving, not tear people down if they have different views and choices. Be proud of what you have

19

accomplished. If you attempted to breastfeed and felt it didn't work for you, that is okay. You did the best you could with the knowledge and support you had at the time. Each drop of breastmilk your child gets is a gift. But if it isn't for you, know that you are still making a positive impact on your child by providing them with the next best thing. You are powerful!

Chapter 2: Anatomy, Hormones, and Baked Brownies

I was raised in an environment where the breast was praised for what it really was designed for—providing the perfect food for a baby. News flash, men—boobies are designed to feed! So if I hear one more time that breastfeeding is sexual or gross or inappropriate, I may just lose my ever-loving mind. Women should not have to cover up when they are feeding their baby! Do we wear a blanket over our heads every time we eat a hamburger? Or go to the bathroom just so we can enjoy a milkshake? Of course not, because feeding/eating is a normal human function.

So let's talk about the anatomy of the breast and how it all works. To really understand the process of milk making, it helps to see how each part of our body works together. Every mother's biggest concern is whether or not she can make enough milk to fully feed her baby. We can see how many ounces we are pumping out, or how much we giving a baby in a bottle, but with the breast we have to trust our bodies. That can be scary, overwhelming, and downright exhausting. But remember, quality is just as important as quantity. Let's start from the beginning, shall we?

When you first become pregnant, your breasts immediately begin the process of prepping for the full-time job of being the ultimate breastaurant. The reason our breasts get tender in the first trimester is because the inside of our breasts are beginning to change and double in size. The inside of the breast looks like broccoli. (I know you will never look at broccoli the same way again. I told my husband that in the middle of dinner and ruined stir fry for him forever.) Think of the nipple as the "stem" and the "flowerettes" as the alveoli or milk ducts. Between ten weeks of pregnancy, your body begins the process of creating colostrum in the "flowerettes" or milk ducts. Colostrum is the very first milk your baby will receive and there is a reason we call it "liquid gold." This thick, sticky, nutrient-rich substance coats the baby's gut to protect against bacteria and infections. It immediately boosts the baby's immune system and reduces inflammation. It also works as a natural laxative to push out your baby's first poop, known as meconium. Meconium is thick, sticky, black-tar poop that has basically been lining the developing digestive tract. When the baby is born and little one begins to suck, the peristalsis of the colon begins, and the colostrum pushes out all the poop/waste that accumulated and replaces it with live protective antibodies. Remember, babies have to "chew to poo." Colostrum is the most important food your baby will ever receive.

You may notice that as your due date approaches (or rather your guess date, because unless you know exactly when "Mr.

Happy" took a swim in your cave of wonder, it is basically a guesstimate), thick sometimes dry yellow droplets will start leaking from your breasts. WOO HOO! That is fantastic! That means your body is getting ready, and your breasts are gearing up for their job. Some women choose to hand express and freeze some of their colostrum to give to baby as an extra supplement in case little one struggles to latch in the beginning. This is not necessary, but can offer some peace of mind for momma. However, nipple stimulation is a powerful tool in causing the uterus to contract, so you may want to avoid hand expression until you get approval from your healthcare team or are at least thirty-eight weeks pregnant.

You may also notice your breasts getting bigger and darker. Your areola and nipple will often double in size and or shape. Nipples are elastic by nature and are capable of stretching up to three times their resting length. So if you were born with flat nipples or inverted nipples (yes, that is a thing; they come in all shapes and sizes), the baby's sucking and the pump will cause them to protrude. Gives new meaning to "Elastagirl" from *The Incredibles*!

We all have a mammary line that starts at our visible nipples and goes all the way down to our feet. In utero, most of the nipples along the mammary line disappear, but you can have a third nipple that lingers along that line. (You all are totally going to go to the mirror and try and find the third nipple now, I am sure of it). Most of the time, it looks like a mole and goes unnoticed. However, sometimes that third nipple will grow and change during pregnancy and may even lactate once baby is here. I have seen them on the tummy and thigh or under the arm. If you are lucky, it is right next to your visible nipples. Bonus boob! Do not panic if you start to lactate in an area of your body that you were not expecting. It won't last long, as there usually is not underlying glandular tissue to support production. It just makes you super unique.

The bumps that are forming on your areola are called Montgomery glands and they serve a very important purpose. Our incredible bodies have a built-in sanitation station. Montgomery glands release a sebaceous oil that sterilizes the breast, cleaning any bacteria, so no need to use soap on your nipples, just water. They also secrete the same scent as amniotic fluid, so to your baby, it literally smells like home. It's like a pan of fresh-baked brownies. The familiar scent helps guide the baby to the area where their food lies. Babies cannot see clearly when they are first born. In fact, they primarily see in black and white. Therefore, they rely on their other senses to guide them through the first three months of life, also known as the fourth trimester.

You have probably also noticed the dark line forming on your belly known as the *linea nigra,* which translates to the "black line." It runs vertically along the midline of the abdomen from the pubic bone to your belly button. The darker your

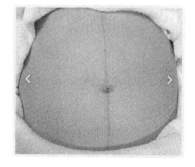

skin is naturally, the darker the streak becomes. This happens as a result of an increase in the melanocyte-stimulating hormone produced by the placenta, which is also the cause of melasma, which is the darkening of the pigment around the edges of the face. The purpose of these pigment changes is to guide the baby to the breast and mom's face. These are natural God-given instincts and characteristics provided by our bodies as a means of survival. The mother-baby dyad is so deeply connected that, even during pregnancy, the mother's body is preparing for the need to feed.

When a baby is first born, providing all goes accordingly, the babe is placed on the mother's abdomen. The mother's body will instantly react, causing a surge of oxytocin (the love hormone), which is responsible for bonding and is crucial in the milk-making process. The mother's body temperature will increase to warm the baby and stabilize the infant's temp and blood sugar. If the baby gets chilled, it can lower the infant's blood sugar, which can be a serious medical crisis. To prevent that, the mother may even spike a fever to help warm her newborn. Pretty incredible how our bodies know how much to love someone we just met.

Newborn babies also have what we call the crawling reflex or step reflex. When baby is placed on his tummy, he literally gets on all fours and crawls up the abdomen, seeking out the breast. Baby will go through nine stages in this process to help guide himself to his food. Essentially, the dark line on your belly (linea nigra) is like the "treasure map" that leads to

25

the "targets" (darkened areola) to where the "baked brownies" are (Montgomery glands). Your baby will use his sense of smell and the contrast in colors of the skin to guide him as he crawls up to the breast, where he roots on the nipple and latches onto the breast all by himself. How freaking cool is that! We really do not have to do anything but leave the kid alone and baby does the rest. What is also interesting is that, while the baby is crawling, the feet are pushing against the top of your uterus, known as the fundus, applying pressure and encouraging contractions to help involute the uterus and birth the placenta. It still blows my mind after all these years of catching babies just how beautifully our bodies come together to heal and create.

The most comfortable way to latch a baby is in the biological nursing position, known as laid back breastfeeding, which is just what was described above. Mom is on her back, reclined, and baby is lying on her chest, using his/her reflexes to allow a deep latch. It may seem awkward at first, but you will soon find that this is truly the easiest way to rest, bond, and feed your little one.

Your mom brain will "think" it is best to bring the breast to the baby, with the baby on his back, however that goes against everything biological. The baby's airway, eustachian tubes, palate, and sinuses are very close together. If you try to latch a baby with her on her back, the tongue will pull back and block the airway, which can cause choking, gulping air, and stridor breathing (that is the squeaky sound you hear when baby is swallowing). Little one has absolutely no control over the flow of the breast, and if you have a fast letdown, she is going to get overwhelmed, which will cause major discomfort for both of you. Not only will the baby become extra gassy, but your nipples will also feel like hamburger. If the baby feels the flow is too fast, he will bite, and you will end up with lipstick nipples. (This is where the nipple looks slanted or tapered like lipstick due to misplaced pressure.) Lipstick is great, but not when it comes to your nipples. OUCH!

The goal is to get the nipple past the soft palate in the baby's mouth so that the lips can flange out like a fish, compressing the ring around the areola, where the nerves that signal the brain to release the hormone to make milk rest. The only time this will be difficult is if the baby has any form of oral tethering or ties, which can make it difficult to create a seal or can otherwise make breastfeeding difficult for the baby. I will cover that extensively in another chapter. It is literally my favorite topic, and I will explain all the ins and outs of it. They call me the "Booby Fairy" for a reason, my friends. I am also going to provide a step-by-step guide on how to latch a baby correctly in the next chapter. Do not worry, girl, I am here to guide you.

Last but not least in our anatomy lesson are the hormones that make this all happen. Prolactin and oxytocin are the two hormones that directly affect breastfeeding and how milk is made. The minute the baby (or the pump) sucks on the nipple, the brain receives a message to begin the process. The anterior lobe of the pituitary gland (a small bean-shaped gland located at the base of our brain, behind our nose and between our ears) begins to produce prolactin. The posterior lobe produces oxytocin.

Prolactin has the awesome job of secreting milk from the cells of the alveoli. Levels of prolactin rise significantly in pregnancy to prepare for breastfeeding after birth. However, the hormone is blocked by progesterone (the pregnancy hormone), powered by your placenta. Once the placenta is delivered, the brain is signaled to bring down the progesterone wall and let prolactin do its thing. This is why we always ask about your vaginal bleeding postpartum if your milk is delayed in coming in, as a retained placenta will prevent the body from making milk. It is kind of like when you are riding Splash Mountain at Disneyland, and right before you're about to make the big drop at the top of the cliff, a wooden wall goes up to stop the flow of water until the last rider has passed. Once the course is clear, the wall drops and your log ride rushes down the drop, creating a bid splash. That is prolactin. This tremendous hormone shift is why you get the baby blues in the first few days postpartum. You are on an emotional roller coaster. Postpartum is grand!

Oxytocin, the love hormone, which we already know is responsible for orgasms and uterine contractions, is also responsible for making the myoepithelial cells around the alveoli contract, allowing the milk ejection reflex to occur.

Oxytocin is triggered by the mother's sensations and feelings. If the nipples are touched, or mom can smell her baby or hear the baby cry, the flood gates open, which is why skin-to-skin contact is so important. Sometimes just thinking about how much she loves her sweet little one is enough to make this happen. This reflex is also known as your milk "letting down." The amount of breast stimulation you get in those first three days determines how much milk you will make for the next three months.

Some women describe the milk ejection reflex as feeling like pins and needles. Others claim it feels like a warm, rushing feeling, while other mommas say that their breasts feel heavy. However, not every woman will feel her milk "letting down," so do not let that scare you if you don't get the warm tingling sensation in your breasts prior. You may simply notice that all of a sudden the baby is gulping or having strong rhythmic jaw movements after around two minutes of sucking, and that is its own sign that the hormone is working. You may also feel sleepy, calm, thirsty, or euphoric. If you instead experience feelings of dread or anxiety when your milk lets down, this could be a sign of a condition called Dysphoric Milk Ejection Reflex, otherwise known as D-MER. There are many reasons for this response, but usually it means that there is an increase in cortisol (stress hormone) or your body is lacking in B vitamins. It does eventually go away, but I strongly recommend seeing an IBCLC if you experience even thirty seconds of feeling melancholy while breastfeeding. I will cover this and other postpartum mood changes in more depth in chapter 13.

Cortisol, our fight-or-flight hormone, is the mortal enemy of oxytocin. Stress is one of the biggest killers of milk supply, as it physically blocks the release. I know—awesome. You just had a baby, and you're sleep deprived. Everyone is telling you how to raise your baby, and your visiting in-laws are trying to do things their way. Your partner feels left out, and your body is recovering from a whirlwind of sensations after having birthed a bowling ball. You are going to be a tad stressed!

SKIN-TO-SKIN CARE

One of the most important ways to combat stress and regulate your hormones and the baby's nervous system is to do skin-to-skin or kangaroo care. This is one of nature's most powerful tools for the initial care of a newborn. The benefits to both mother and baby are numerous, and in many scenarios proves to be lifesaving.

Skin-to-skin care is when a mother and baby are cuddled up together, with a baby lying shirt-free on her mother's bare chest. The American Academy of Pediatrics Policy Statement on Breastfeeding states: "Healthy infants should be placed and remain in direct skin-to-skin contact with their mothers immediately after delivery until the first feeding is accomplished."[1]

So why is this simple post-delivery step so important? Your baby has just undergone a huge change, and is going to need some time to adjust from "womb to room." Skin-to-skin care allows this to happen in a less traumatic way. As I mentioned, a mother's body will rise in temperature to meet the needs of her fragile newborn, and so a mother's chest is a far better infant warmer than our synthetic ones. This simple step provides a gentler transition to life outside of the womb immediately

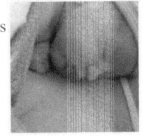

Alyssa 24hrs old

after birth. Beyond the initial transition that occurs, there are also many medical benefits for both mother and baby.

BENEFITS TO BABY

- Stabilizes the baby's breathing pattern and oxygen intake
- Maintains infant temperature better than an infant warmer, allowing the baby to stay warmer
- Stabilizes glucose levels, preventing hypoglycemia (low blood sugar), which can be triggered by low body temperature
- Reduces stress hormones released from crying due to an immediate separation from mother. Babies placed skin-to-skin cry less and calm more easily
- Stabilizes baby's blood pressure

- Increases early breastfeeding initiation
- Decreases risk of jaundice
- Increases weight gain
- Strengthens infant brain development through verbal and tactile stimulation
- Decreases pain perception during newborn procedures such as heel sticks and vitamin K injections. Most newborn procedures and assessments can be done while baby is still skin-to-skin on the mother.

BENEFITS TO MOM
- Triggers release of oxytocin, which has a relaxing calming effect, promoting mother/infant bonding while also stimulating milk production
- Enhances the birth experience
- Increases breast milk production (at any age)
- Increases duration and success of breastfeeding
- Increases confidence in parenting

BENEFITS TO BREASTFEEDING
Studies have shown time and time again that breast milk is the best source of food for all infants. An article in the *Journal of Midwifery and Women's Health*[2] showed the results of a randomized controlled trial of very early mother-infant skin-to-skin contact. The study was done to evaluate the effects of skin-to-skin contact during the first two hours

post birth compared to the standard care of holding a baby wrapped in a blanket, and the effects it had on long-term breastfeeding outcomes. The results were astonishing.

A baby is most responsive to cues from their mothers in the first two hours of life. It is known as a "sensitive period" and is the most crucial step for establishing effective breastfeeding. The results showed that when babies are placed directly on their mother's chest, it triggers a catecholamine surge that results in achieving effective breastfeeding sooner. They also showed fewer long-term breastfeeding problems than the babies who were NOT placed skin-to-skin but simply put in a synthetic environment wrapped in a blanket.

For premature babies in the neonatal intensive care unit, skin-to-skin contact can prove to be lifesaving. The close contact stabilizes the infant's body heat as well as their neurological system. It is one of the greatest gifts that these fragile babies can receive to help fight off infection after an already compromised start. It is as close as these babies can get to being placed back in the womb.

The great thing about skin-to-skin care is that it can be done as often as mother and baby like. In addition, the mother's partner can also participate in this special bonding time as well. I went back to work when Alyssa was six weeks old, and Ryan was terrified, as she would cry every time he held her. Of course she did! He was tense, and she fed off that tension. So I immediately told him to take his shirt off, place her in just a diaper, and snuggle her in. He was convinced she was going to pull his chest hair and try to latch on…which she totally did. It was hilarious! However, as soon as he was able to feel her and smell her, he relaxed and she relaxed. Before you know it, both were snoring while watching a football game. Skin-to-skin contact is the single most powerful neurological calming technique there is.

Take the time to invest in each other. It is a special moment that should be enjoyed. You are giving both yourself, your milk supply, and most importantly your baby a wonderful start in life.

Take each day as it comes. I can almost guarantee that as soon as you tackle one obstacle, another will arrive. Being a mother is the most time consuming, exhausting, rewarding, confusing, amazing thrill ride you will ever embark on. Take those hormone swings as they come. Your body has just gone through one hell of a fight, and your hormones are raging, but you got this!

Chapter 3: Reflexes, Pressure Points, Positions

I have had the unique opportunity to work in a hospital setting, a pediatric office, and a private outpatient practice. In the hospital when the IBCLC lactation consultant comes in to help with the baby, there is one goal: latch the baby, check the box, move on. There is no time for good solid education, no time to sit and truly listen to the mother's concerns, and certainly no time to truly watch and check the baby's suck ability. So much goes into breastfeeding education and a true consult, but to be brutally honest, that just isn't realistic for the hospital IBCLC. I remember having six hours in my shift to see eighteen babies. There was no room for education and support, and I couldn't time my visits to feeding times for all those little ones, all while coordinating with the nurses' exams and helping mom get some sleep. It truly is bonkers to me how much gets missed in those first few moments.

Every twelve hours, someone new enters the room, with a new opinion, a new set of tricks, and hopefully up-to-date experience. The biggest complaint I hear from both the new mother and the hospital staff is the inconsistency of information provided. When that nurse or IBCLC went to school, and how much hands-on training they have had, truly impacts how effective the care they provide will be. It is like the game of telephone. We start with the same goal, but somewhere along the journey, the point gets lost in translation. It wasn't until I left the hospital that I realized that everything we do to help you in the hospital backfires the minute you go home.

In the hospital, the nurses typically position the baby in a football hold since it is, to be honest, easier on them. Initially, in a hospital bed with a gazillion pillows, you will have success latching. It may not feel right or look right, but if baby is swallowing they count it as a win. Then you go home and try to sit in a chair with a sore bottom. You organize your "pillow table," which just falls everywhere. You end up hunched over your baby, wincing with pain and gritting your teeth as your baby latches on in a backwards, half-misunderstood football hold that ends up killing your back and destroying your nipples. Sounds super fun, huh?

New mothers go into breastfeeding with the expectation that it is supposed to hurt. You have heard time and time again from your great aunt Suzie to just toughen up those nipples. Soon you will have a callous and it won't hurt…just wait it out for several weeks. I remember my mom telling me to use a washcloth to roughen up my nipples before the baby got here so they were ready for the damage. Ummm….I don't know about you, but that sounds horrendous to me! Why would anyone want to torture themselves for weeks with unbearable nipple pain that leads to infections, depression, and grumpy babies?

Ladies, let me tell you… IT IS NOT SUPPOSED TO HURT TO BREASTFEED! I know, I know… most of you are looking at me like I have three heads, but it is true. Feeding your baby is not meant to be painful, but it often is. If it is painful, that means that something needs to be adjusted. YOU DO NOT HAVE TO LIVE WITH THAT PAIN FOR WEEKS ON END! If your baby is gassy, biting, crying, or looks like he is "falling asleep" on the job, which in my opinion is basically the baby playing opossum, something needs to be adjusted. Too often we women grin and bear it, and end up quitting far sooner than was needed. There is a way, and I am going to teach you. Some people call it the "Gauss Method." Some just think I am sprinkling Booby Fairy dust, which is AWESOME. But all I am doing is honoring the baby's pressure points and reflexes. If we stop and listen to both of your instincts, feeding gets a whole lot easier. Let me break it down for you.

First, before you can latch your baby without pain, you have to understand the baby's natural reflexes. Your little one is born with seventy-five natural reflexes that help aid in their survival. Not all of those pertain to feeding, and I do not want to overwhelm you, so I will focus on the ten that primarily have to do with breastfeeding.

There also are twelve cranial nerves that are responsible for initiating most of the baby's reflexes. These nerves are super sensitive, which is why you never hold or compress the top of their head when latching. This will cause discomfort for them and most likely end with junior biting you. If there is too much pressure on the head, baby will pull back, cry, and probably not want to latch. I won't bore you with the details about these nerves, as that could be a whole chapter in itself. However, if you are a science nerd like me, I have put a list of books that may interest you in the back of this book.

There are ten reflexes that pertain to a baby's latch.

Reflexes

1. **Crawling reflex** – This is present from birth and is used to initiate the journey to the breast. After birth, when the baby is placed on the mother's chest, he will get on all fours and literally crawl to the breastaurant. This lasts for about two weeks.

2. **Sucking reflex** – Present as early as twenty-four weeks of gestation. When the soft palate is stimulated, the infant extends the tongue over the lower gum, raises the jaw, and pulls the nipple into the mouth. This is almost an obligatory response by the baby to suck on anything in the mouth for the first three months of life. At that point it turns from an automatic response to a voluntary response.

3. **Rooting reflex** – Stimulated by touch to the face or the mouth, it causes the baby to turn

towards the breast, open the mouth, extend the tongue, and grasp the breast. This is seen as early as thirty-two weeks of gestation, is strongest at forty weeks, and usually fades around three months of age.

4. **Suck/swallow/breathe reflex** – Swallowing has been observed as early as twelve weeks' gestation in utero, as the baby learns from routine swallowing of amniotic fluid. (Basically the baby drinks and pees amniotic fluid throughout the pregnancy. Kinda like sitting in his own sterile cesspool. Do not worry, amniotic fluid is filtered out daily, which is one reason why you pee so often. Hooray!) More than forty muscles work together to coordinate the movement of air and food through the oral cavity. These muscles work in harmony to control lip movement and jaw glides and to influence the shape and action of the tongue and cheeks. They also elevate the soft palate to protect the airway. At thirty-nine weeks, the sulcai of the brain (that is the "wrinkles" in the brain) is finally developed enough to coordinate all three motions in fine unity. This is why if the baby has any form of oral tethering in the tongue, lip, or cheeks, it makes it extremely difficult for the baby to eat without coughing, choking, breathing, or sucking in air.

5. **Open hand posture** – Your baby will communicate to you through many cues, but watching your baby's hands can tell you quite a bit. At the beginning of the feed, the hand will be clenched in a fist.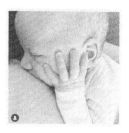

Towards the end of the feed, when baby is becoming full, his hand will open completely with an open palm. That is how you know when baby is done.

6. **Cough reflex** – This is one of baby's most important reflexes. This happens when anything enters the airway or is aspirated. The sensory response in the larynx (that is the flap of tissue that covers the windpipe, kinda like a kazoo) causes a constriction of the airway, pausing breathing and allowing the baby to cough or propel the substance from the airway. This protective response is almost automatic, but depends on the maturity of the infant. A preterm baby may not have the strength and ability to cough and then breathe quickly, and apnea can occur. This is usually temporary, but is definitely scary for momma.

7. **Gag reflex** – This reflex is very strong at birth. Its severity depends on the structure of the

40

tongue. Usually this is triggered from pressure on the very back of the tongue. If the baby has a posterior or submucosal posterior tongue tie, this reflex will be especially strong.

8. **Tongue thrust** – This reflex usually lasts till about four to six months and is triggered by stimulation of the lips, causing the tongue to thrust out any foreign substance. You may notice this happen with pacifiers and bottle nipples if the baby is done. Once this reflex fades, the baby is usually ready to start solids.

9. **Phasic bite** – This is the rhythmic opening and closing of the jaw when the gums are exposed and goes hand in hand with both transverse tongue and thrust reflex. If you rub your young one's lower gumline (which they LOVE, by the way), you will see the lateral side of the tongue move from side to side. If this is difficult, it may be an indication of a posterior tongue tie.

10. **Transverse tongue** – This happens when the side of the tongue is stroked, causing the tongue to move forward. This is different than the gag reflex, which is triggered by the anterior or front of the tongue being stroked.

I know that all may sound super overwhelming and confusing, but understanding what reactions are normal or abnormal when it comes to the infant's airway and breathing is crucial for deciphering the possibility of an anatomical abnormality of the tongue, lips, and palate. You will find yourself staring at your little one, scanning for any changes, any new developments. Remember, you will know your baby better than any doctor, nurse, lactation consultant, grandparent, or auntie. If you feel something isn't right, you are most likely correct. Trust your gut!

Now that you have the mouth reflexes down, next you have to understand the five pressure points on a baby that initiate a positive latch. I am very big on honoring the baby's pressure points. These areas are sensitive and responsive for a reason, and when you work *with* the baby, listening to their cues, you will be far more successful in your feeding journey. Using acupressure is a safe and effective way to help ease pain and discomfort, while also boosting the immune system and digestive tract. So let us break them down:

Pressure Points

1. **Nipple on the philtrum** (that is the cupid bow above your upper lip) Du 26 – This is one of the most powerful points. It is as strong as a knee-jerk reaction. When you rest the nipple on the cupid bow, that baby will immediately open her mouth wide, and tilt the head back. This will allow you to then guide the baby's mouth up and over the nipple and areola by resting the bottom lip at

the base and scooping the mouth over. I often see mothers trying to tickle the bottom lip of the baby with their nipple, or dragging it from nose to chin, but all that does is act like a dangling carrot. The baby will try searching for it, but if the target is constantly moving, he will either bite or shut down, after waving his gaping mouth from side to side. Your instinct will then be to bring the breast to the baby, all while your critter is a moving, screaming target. It does not work and it absolutely is not comfy. Remember: "Nose, bows, chin first it goes." Rest the nipple below the nose, on the cupid bow. When baby opens wide, rest the chin on the breast and bring baby's mouth up, over, and in.

2. **Pressure in between the shoulder blades** – This point is known in Chinese medicine as Du 12. This area is considered to be one of the most calming points for babies and children. When latching, apply light pressure in this area or rub in a circular motion to centralize the nervous system so the baby can be calm and focused while eating. Make sure that you are not putting any  pressure on the baby's head, specifically behind

the ears, as that can trigger the phasic bite reflex, causing pain for both of you.

3. **Pressure on the butt** – The Du pressure point is located between the coccyx (tailbone) and the anus (bum hole). This 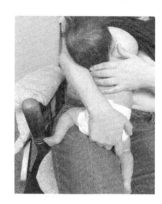 point is used to calm the spirit, which is often why patting a little one's butt invokes a calming effect. This is more to guide the baby to stay turned toward momma. If there is not firm pressure on the shoulder, butt, and feet, baby will think he is falling and will either bite or come off completely. Creating a firm "back board" with your arm gently placed along the spine and butt of baby immediately places your critter in a more focused, centered neurological space.

4. **Pressure between the second and third toe** – The tips of the toes are related to the hypothalamus, which helps 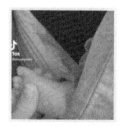 to regulate hunger and stimulate appetite. We all know that when it is time to eat, baby will let you know IT IS TIME TO EAT!

Gentle pressure and tapping on the toes will help ease the pangs of hunger as your little one sucks to encourage your milk to let down. If you also press on the webbing between the second and third toe, it will make the baby suck. Remember babies have to "chew to poo," so this not only helps baby to instantly suck rhythmically, it also aids in helping your critter to poop.

5.   Pressure on the roof of the mouth on the palate – This is the other magic poop button. This spot elicits the sucking reflex and creates peristalsis of the colon. I would say nine out of ten times when I am doing a suck assessment on a baby, the minute my finger hits the soft curve of the palate, boom… baby poop. This is the exact reason I wear  scrubs. Hey if I am not getting peed, pooped, or puked on, I am not doing my job.

Babies are so aware. It truly is awe inspiring to watch them develop and see how every intricate cell of their body works together to create the perfect environment for survival. Now that you have a better understanding of how the baby's body works in regards to latching, you can understand the many options for breastfeeding positions.

My best advice for positioning is to find one that works with the baby, and with your breast. If it isn't broken, you don't need to fix it. If you honor the baby's pressure points and anatomy, it won't necessarily matter how you hold the baby. However, if something does not feel right, de-latch and try again.

The most common positions you will see or read about are:

1. **Football Hold** – This is one of the more popular positions demonstrated in the hospital by the nurses. It gets its name because you are literally holding the baby on his back, tucked in like a football. I personally never recommend this position unless the baby has a severe case of torticollis (crooked neck) and does not yet have the  ability to move his head in both directions. Torticollis is when the baby's head is tilted to one side, or he has a "kink" in his neck, making it painful and difficult to rotate in both directions. This can be caused by a tongue tie pulling the ligaments to one side or a traumatic birth, but could also be due to how the baby was positioned in the uterus. You will find that most nurses prefer this

position when helping with breastfeeding as it is easier from their perspective to latch the

baby for you. In a hospital bed, you are reclined with a crazy amount of pillows that create the ultimate pillow nest. The nurse essentially latches the baby for you without any help. I find however that this often sets mom up for failure when she gets home. You do not have the same set up and therefore end up leaning forward, which is painful for both you and baby. The only way a football hold can be helpful is if the baby is turned into your side, and you are reclined with the baby coming towards the breast.

2. **Cross Cradle Hold**

This is my personal favorite and what I demonstrate with most of my patients. I find it the easiest to manage, and it makes it easy to support the baby's back and neck. In this position, the mother's arm forms a back board around baby's back as mentioned above and brings the baby across mother's abdomen. The other hand goes under your breast and holds the breast like a "U" shape. This allows the dominant arm to fully support the responsive pressure points and guide the baby in.

3. **Cradle Hold** – This is pretty standard to what you see pictured in most breastfeeding images. The mom is literally cradling the baby, with one arm on the back, and the baby's head resting in the crook of the elbow. I recommend this for older babies, with stronger head control. As long as the baby is able to lie tummy to tummy, this will be a very  soothing position. However, it is important that you make sure that the baby's head is not tilted too much to one side, as this can cause some nipple damage.

4. **Koala Hold** – Around sixteen weeks (if you're like me and don't math well, that's four months), the koala hold becomes super helpful. During this stage of development, the baby's eye development has strengthened, and she is able to see things more clearly. This is also the age of discovery, which can make breastfeeding rather challenging. Baby will latch, suck a couple of times, then get distracted, turning their head in the

opposite direction and taking your nipple with them. OUCH! This is all normal behavior, but it can be quite painful and frustrating as feeding sessions can last longer than needed. The koala hold is an awesome option for the smart, curious critter. In this position, the

baby will straddle your legs, either kneeling or sitting on your thigh or straddling your waist, and then come straight onto the breast. Instead of making the "U" shape you will switch to a classic "C" hold and allow the baby to latch, sitting up, leaning into you. This can also be helpful for a baby who is suffering from GERD, more commonly known as acid reflux. Sitting up will help the baby not vomit or arch as much, which in turn makes feeding much easier for both of you.

5. **Side Lying** – This is when mom is lying in

bed, on her side, and bringing baby to her breast in a side lying position. For example, the baby can be turned in facing mom, latched onto the breast closest to the mattress. Mother can choose to use a rolled blanket or her arm to brace the baby's back. I do not recommend having the baby on his back with his head turned. This can cause the baby to choke or clamp down on the nipple, resulting in a shallow latch and rather sore nipples. When done correctly, side lying can result in some very restful breastfeeding. Both mom and baby are able to breastfeed while sleeping, which is always a beautiful thing. Believe it or not, breastfeeding moms get more sleep than bottle-feeding moms, just for the sheer fact of being able to lie down. Whoop whoop! Let's hear it for the sleep!

6. **Laid Back Nursing** – Last but certainly not least is one of my favorite positions, known as biological laid back nursing. The reason I love this so is because it uses every pressure point and reflex to help baby latch all on his own. This is hands down the most comfortable breastfeeding position  because gravity is able to aid in the extension of the baby's tongue. If mom happens to have a fast letdown, this is also helpful in allowing the baby to control the flow instead of being drenched with

a downpour of milk. When your milk lets down, it is a trickle versus a hose. This is also a safe and comfortable way to sleep while breastfeeding. With the baby's tongue extending down, the airway is freer.

Moms often worry that the baby can't breathe in this position, but the beautiful thing is that babies do not have cartilage in their noses like we do, so the baby can adjust themselves if needed and breathe out the side of the nose. Babies are obligatory nose breathers. If the baby is breathing through their mouth, that is a concern that something else, such as a tongue tie, may be present. I do not recommend creating an air pocket by placing your finger under their nose, as this will cause the nipple to angle up into the palate and that, my friends, is how you get clamped lipstick nipples.

If you are worried about the little one's breathing, I recommend holding the "U" or the "taco" hold so that there is even pressure around the baby's nose and mouth. This way the nipple will be able to go past the palate and not get compressed. Stripes are fashionable, but not when they are on your nipples.

Now that you have a visual on all the positions, reflexes, and pressure points, I give you what I call "The Gauss Method" written out step by step. Take this with you to the hospital, pin it next to your nursing chair, and put it in your phone or wherever your sweet sleep-deprived eyes will be so that you can latch your baby well, with hopefully no pain. Remember, it is not supposed to hurt. If you follow all these steps and there is still pain, then make an appointment with a trained IBCLC. Make sure they are internationally board certified. There are women who claim to be breastfeeding consultants that are not licensed, or have only gone through a basic three-month program. You always want to make sure that you are being cared for by someone with full training and a board certification. Most feeding specialists can offer some form of support, but if you suspect something more complicated, seek out the help of someone licensed. I have included a guide to choosing a lactation consultant in the appendix of this book.

Without further ado, here are your step-by-step instructions for latching your sweet new angel.

THE GAUSS METHOD OF LATCHING

Massage breasts prior to feed (shake the girls). This will help get the milk flowing. Feed on demand eight or more times in twenty-four hours, every two to three hours in the day, every three to four hours at night till baby is past birth weight. Be a baby watcher, not a clock watcher. Babies go through growth spurts at three weeks, six weeks, nine weeks, three months, six months, and nine months, so you may have to adjust your feeding at those times. Listen to your baby's cues. When latching your baby, you want to "Do the Du," meaning you activate all three of the Du acupressure points with each latch. Using acupressure with positioning will decrease inflammation and centralize the nervous system. Okay, let's get started.

1. Use good pillow support (My Breast Friend is my recommendation) up high and right under the breast. If you don't like pillows or can't access this one, remember that as long as baby has pressure on the back and butt you can lean back and allow them to lie on top of your chest. Find something to support your arms so that gravity does not win.

2. Lean back and put your feet up. If your feet are elevated and you start reclined, it will be much harder to bring the breast to the baby, which is the opposite of what you want to do.

3. BRING BABY TO YOU! Do *not* go to the baby!

4. Do the Du. Put your arm around baby's back, creating a back board, and support the head, being cautious not to put too much pressure behind the ears or onto the top of the head. Apply pressure on the Du point in between the shoulder blades with the palm of

your hand. The baby's head should rest in the curve of your hand so you still have control and support. Your elbow should be able to scoop in and support the baby bum, activating the Du 2 point.

5. With the other hand in the shape of a "U," ridge your breast like a taco. Rest nipple on baby's upper lip (cupid bow), activating point Du26. Do not drag your nipple up and down like a dangling carrot. Just rest it on the cupid bow till baby opens wide.

6. When you see baby open, use the hand supporting her neck and head and bring her to you, chin/lower lip on breast, then up and in. Remember the saying: "Nose, bows, up she goes."

7. Cheek should be touching the breast. You should not see the areola from your perspective. Ear, shoulder, hip should be in line.

8. Make sure the bottom hand/arm of the baby is under the breast, hugging in. Do not trap arm down towards baby's side, as this will cause him to bite.

9. Make sure baby is tummy to tummy. It should not hurt. If it hurts, do not grin and bear it. De-latch and try again. The more he is on your belly and you are on your back, the easier it gets. Place a rolled blanket under baby's head for added support.

10. For women who are especially "blessed" with larger pendulous breasts, a rolled burp cloth under the breast to prop it up will help aid in latching.

11.   Allow baby to soften one side and burp, then offer the other. Watch for jaw glides, meaning that the baby's lower jaw will rhythmically glide across the breast and nipple, removing milk. When the large jaw glides stop and baby flutters his mouth, he may be done.

12.   Watch his hands for guidance. If the baby's hand is closed in a fist, he is still hungry. When the hand is open palmed and relaxed, that means baby is satiated.

13.   If desired, you may use the "U" shaped "taco" hand to cradle the baby. If so, massage your pinky finger, (SI1) at the lower left corner of the nail bed in a circular motion while feeding or pumping to increase your letdown. This is an acupressure point that releases a prolactin response and will help with improve milk let down.

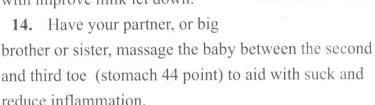

14.   Have your partner, or big brother or sister, massage the baby between the second and third toe (stomach 44 point) to aid with suck and reduce inflammation.

Breastfeeding is a learned art. Sometimes it takes a few attempts to get it right. Enjoy the moment, take deep breaths, drink some water, and remember that YOU GOT THIS!

Chapter 4: What a Pain in the Ducts

Sore nipples are the absolute worst! It truly is toe-curling pain. I have a high pain tolerance (my husband may think otherwise), but when it comes to nipple pain, there are no words. I would much rather give birth to triplets without an epidural than deal with the stinging, soul-crushing pain that is a cracked nipple. The only thing worse is a bad case of mastitis. If you have been there, you know exactly what I am talking about. It is a flu in your boob. The things we women go through for our children! And you know what? I would do it again and again and again.

As a mom, I am willing to take one for the team, grin and bear it, as my gorgeous little piranha sucks the life out of me. I truly think that this is why women wait so long to get help. We are told it is supposed to hurt, and before you know it— boom—the nipple that once was round has now been smushed like a pancake with a constant crease, or been compressed to forever be shaped like lipstick. What…in… the…actual…hell?! Nope, nope, nope. Ladies, I have said it once before and I am going to say it again even louder: BREASTFEEDING IS NOT SUPPOSED TO HURT. However, it often does, and when it does that means something needs to be adjusted. It also means that you need to get the help of an IBCLC that can assess just what is going on.

Your nipples are not used to getting that much action (at least I don't think they are) and will therefore have a bit of chapping. Putting some expressed breast milk on your nipples with some coconut oil will help soothe them. However, if it exceeds minor chapping and becomes bleeding scabs, or you are pumping out blood, we need to talk. If your breast has turned hot and red or lumpy, we also need to talk.

Sore nipples and overall breast pain can be due to several different issues such as clogged ducts, milk bleb, mastitis, Raynaud's, thrush, bacterial infections, vasospasm, even pump trauma. I am going to break them down for you so if you experience any form of pain throughout your journey, you will know the warning signs to look for along with a few at-home remedies to treat yourself. Let's start with the basics:

1. BLEEDING, CRACKED NIPPLES

No one loves this, but it will likely happen to some degree. The main reason this happens is a shallow latch and poor positioning. Next feed, go through my latching method and see if baby is in a line, tummy to tummy, you are leaning back, and you do not see your areola. If you see areola, the latch is too shallow and this will cause pain. If the baby is even slightly on his back, this can cause pinching and pain.

If your nipple gets trapped between the baby's soft palate and his tongue, a compression will happen. Repeat trauma in the same position for hours will result in the crack opening up over and over. It is essential to fix the position as best you can, or seek the help of an IBCLC to determine if there is an oral tie present. The sooner the better.

If latching the baby is just too painful because of the abrasions, it is perfectly fine to use a nipple shield, as long as it is put on correctly, or simply pump and bottle-feed until the trauma has healed. Babies do not get nipple confusion; they have flow preference. It is incredibly important that you keep the breast empty as we do not want that turning into an infection.

A nipple shield is a small, thin silicone device that fits over the nipple and areola during breastfeeding. It acts as a barrier

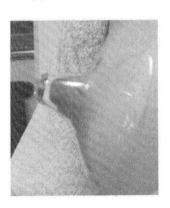

Nipple Shields used for flat, inverted, sore nipples

between the baby's mouth and your breast. It looks very similar to a hat—some moms call it the "sombrero" or "witches' hat." It works by vacuuming the nipple and part of the areola in to create a sort of suction. Contrary to older versions that were much thicker, this product is made of a light clear silicone, with four holes at the tip for milk to flow. I only recommend using a Medela brand

24mm nipple shield. Other brands and other sizes can cause more discomfort and allow for a decrease in supply. The shields come in extra small (16mm), small (20mm), and medium (24mm). Rarely will anyone need a small or extra small size. I cannot stress enough the importance of using the correct size. The majority of women will need a 24mm medium size to adequately suction in the nipple and areola into the shield to allow for milk transfer. The exception to this rule would be if the mother's nipple truly measures 16mm or less, or the baby is a preterm infant. Studies have shown that the use of a nipple shield with a preterm infant does allow for more milk to transfer until the suck swallow reflex kicks in around the thirty-nine week gestation mark. The suction allows the baby to transfer the milk correctly.

The nipple shield was originally designed to help women with flat and inverted nipples be able to breastfeed, however it is NOT a breast shell, which is worn during pregnancy or in-between feeds to elongate the nipple to make it easier for the baby to grasp. Breast shells are contraindicated now and should not be used, in my opinion, for sore nipples, or inverted nipples.

For some women, the only way they will ever be able to breastfeed is with a nipple shield, where for others it is just a temporary solution. There is nothing wrong with using a nipple shield as long as it is placed and used correctly. My take on the subject has always been that if it helps the mother and the baby maintain a good breastfeeding relationship, and it is not affecting the milk supply, there is nothing wrong with using one.

In most cases the nipple shield will only be used for a week to ten days. If you use one for longer than two weeks, your baby may become accustomed to the texture and shape, and it may take some time to wean off of the shield. In most cases I have seen, the baby at some point weans themself off the shield. One moment they will be nursing beautifully with it, and then the next moment they knock it off. Every baby is different, and every mother's nipples are different. Most inverted nipples eventually do come out with time, but initially the constriction of tissue can be painful. Being flexible and having lots of patience are key when it comes to breastfeeding. If you decide to continue using the nipple shield, here are some recommended guidelines:

A. BEFORE USE: Always be sure to wash the shield in between uses with warm, soapy water. Rinse and dry. Prior to attaching, use some hand expression to help stimulate milk flow and evert your nipple as much as possible.

B. HOW TO APPLY: Make sure the shield is dry prior to applying. Do not place lanolin or oil on the shield in hopes that it will help it "stick." Invert the shield slightly before placing on breast. Do NOT completely turn it inside out. Make sure the cut out notch is facing the direction that the baby's nose will turn. With the shield slightly inverted, place at the base of your nipple and stretch it over your nipple. This should allow for a good amount of suction, and your nipple should pull out on its own. If needed, use your finger to help pop out the nipple. It is normal for there to be a gap between the end of your nipple and the end of the shield.

C. HOW TO USE: Once the shield is on correctly, follow the steps previously mentioned in chapter 3 to latch. Observe that the baby's mouth is open wide and the lips are flanged like a fish. The lips and cheeks should be touching the breast rather than sliding back and forth on the shield.

D. Listen for audible swallowing and watch for jaw glides. The baby's mouth should remain open and wide and the lower jaw should be gliding in a rhythmic motion, not sliding back and forth on the shield.

E. Watch your baby's cues for signs that the breast has emptied. The baby will either de-latch on their own, or the audible swallowing and jaw glides will stop. Breast compression while baby is nursing is extremely important, as this will encourage your baby to suck vigorously while also effectively empty the breast and stimulating the breast to produce more milk for the next feed. This will also prevent any disruption to your supply.

F. AFTER FEEDING: Observe if your baby is content, if your breasts feel softer, and that milk is present in the shield. These are all signs of good milk transfer. If you have concerns that the nipple shield is hindering your milk supply, or you are unsure if your baby is getting enough, consider a visit with your lactation consultant, who can weigh the baby before and after a feed to see just how much of that precious milk he drank. Remember, if you baby is gaining weight and has an adequate number of pees and poops, you are doing a great job feeding your little one! Weight checks at a breastfeeding support group or at your pediatrician may be recommended periodically to make sure your baby is maintaining and growing well.

G. When you feel ready to get rid of the shield, gradually begin to remove the shield with each feeding session. A great way to do this would be to start a feed with the nipple shield, and then halfway through, or when it is time to switch to the next breast, remove the shield and attempt to latch. Sometimes if you try to remove the shield at the beginning of a feed when the baby is most hungry, the baby will not be willing to cooperate. It's best to wait till their little belly is slightly full before attempting something new. If it doesn't work the first time, be patient. Place the baby on your chest, skin to skin. Eventually your baby will reorient and before you know it she will be feeding just as well without the shield as she did with it.

If there is blood in the milk (we refer to that as strawberry milk; I know…gross) it is safe for the baby to drink. Some mothers, however, have a hard time giving visible blood to their baby, and I totally get that. It is also okay for baby to drink straight from the breast if there is bleeding as well. The suction from the baby and the soothing medicinal aspect of the milk will most likely help stop the bleeding. Just a warning about their poop. If the baby has ingested blood, it will appear like coffee grounds in their poop. Bright red blood in baby poop is a different problem entirely, and you should consult with your pediatrician. Usually it is just an anal fissure (small tear around the rectum), or it could be due to sensitivity to a food such as dairy or soy. Either way, I recommend taking one of the bloody diapers into the pediatrician's office to be tested.

So how do you treat and heal bleeding nipples? Here are some of the best remedies:

-**Expressed breast milk**. I do not recommend the old-school thought of letting them air dry. I mean, I am all for letting the girls fly free, but the idea of air healing already cracked/chapped nipples is pretty archaic. If breast milk does not work, the following products are most helpful.

- **Hydrogel pads**. I recommend either Soothie by Lansinoh or ComfortGel by Ameda. I personally am not a fan of Medela brand hydrogels. They can almost irritate more than heal, you have to remember to get them wet, and you always have to wipe off the gel prior to feeding. With all hydrogel brands, take the plastic protective covering off and place the sticky gel side over the damaged nipple. The fabric side goes towards your bra. I have seen mommas put the fabric side on their nipple and wonder why it hurts. This probably goes without saying, but sleep-deprived moms will do the craziest things. YIKES!

- **Ointments** (nipple butter, coconut oil). I do not recommend using any brand of lanolin, as this can actually cause increased irritation. If wool sweaters make you itchy, so will the lanolin, which is basically pure wool. Nothing worse than putting something you are allergic to on an already-sensitive area. Plus, studies have shown that lanolin can harvest bacteria, not to mention it stains everything. Whichever ointment you choose, it should be organic so that any residue will not harm the baby if accidentally ingested.

- **Silverette cup**s. Although this is the most expensive option, it is one of the more effective options. Silverettes are small cups crafted out of 925 sterling silver that fit over and help to protect nipples while breastfeeding. These cups feel amazing! Silver has been found to be a natural antimicrobial, anti-fungal, and antibacterial metal that also contains anti-inflammatory agents. It heals and prevents cuts, wounds, cracks, soreness, and infections. They are pretty incredible, but cost around $50. However, I have known moms to take them afterwards and turn them into jewelry. Best of both worlds, I suppose.

2. ENGORGEMENT

Waking up with rock-hard Dolly Parton boobs can be quite shocking, and incredibly painful, but typically there will be some time in your breastfeeding journey that you will end up engorged! One word…owie! Engorgement is what happens to your breasts when there is a sudden rush of hormones triggering a mass production of milk, which gets trapped within the breast tissue prior to removal. It is most common around three to six days after the birth of your baby after this hormone shift has begun to change the composition of your breast milk from the thick colostrum to a more mature milk. Your breasts may feel swollen, fuller, and heavier. In some cases, your breasts might be warm to the touch and appear hard and shiny. You might even begin to notice some reddening of the skin as the tissue stretches. Some women may get a slight fever and experience chills and nausea for a few hours.

Your breasts are trying to figure out how much milk to make for your baby, so they begin by making an overabundant amount. Look at your boobs being overachievers already! In some cases, the engorgement is severe, which causes breast pain and latching difficulties. They are so hard that the baby is unable to latch on. If you think about it, it would be like your baby trying to latch on to an overfilled water balloon that feels more like a bowling ball! The good news is there are steps to take to help ease this discomfort.

Steps To Take To Prevent Engorgement

- Follow the baby's cues for feeding on demand. When the baby exhibits a feeding cue, place him on the breast. Your baby should feed a minimum of eight times, and preferably twelve times, in twenty-four hours. Feeding early and feeding often will help to make sure good milk transfer is occurring.

- Signs that your baby is transferring milk are: audible swallowing, sustained sucking pattern with good jaw glides, pausing and self-starting by the infant, softening of the breast.

- Feed the baby until she self-detaches, generally around fifteen minutes per breast (the time may vary based on the age and oral function of the baby). Allow the baby to empty each breast as best as possible.

▪   Provide breast compressions during each feeding session to help aid in milk removal.

▪   If the breasts do not feel soft, or the baby has only nursed on one side, pump or hand express for no more than ten minutes to relieve the fullness. This will aid is comfort but also signal to your brain to continue to produce more milk for your baby.

Steps For Hard Painful Breasts And Latching Problems Associated With Engorgement

▪   If milk is not flowing well, apply a cold compress to the breasts for fifteen to twenty minutes prior to feeding. Never apply ice directly to the skin. Place a towel or receiving blanket in between. You can use a package of frozen peas or make an "ice diaper" for icing. To do this, saturate one of your baby's newborn diapers, then place it in the freezer. The diaper will freeze and, voila, you have a self-made non-leaking ice pack that contours perfectly to your breast. Side note: they also make awesome ice packs for your rather sore perineum.

▪   Place one hand on the top of the breast and the other on the bottom of the breast and massage in a clockwise motion, pushing excess fluids towards the lymphatic system

- Massage the breasts gently from the chest wall toward the nipple area to help relax the breast tissue and increase the milk flow.

- If the areola is so hard that the baby is unable to latch deeply onto the breast, hand express or pump for about five minutes to soften the areola. To hand express, place your thumb and index finger halfway between the nipple and areola. Gently push in, applying pressure as you roll your fingers out towards the chest wall, and then squeeze in, rolling the fingers back down towards the nipple. Repeat until soft. Having the baby latch more deeply will help to prevent sore, damaged nipples. In some cases, a nipple shield may be helpful.

- It is normal for you to only be able to pump out a small amount of milk from each breast at this time. The majority of the fullness is due to the excess blood and fluids that settled into the breast tissue and which obviously cannot be expressed out.

- If milk is flowing, take a hot shower and allow the warm water to flow over the engorged breasts. The moist heat will encourage the milk to flow faster. Perform breast massage and hand expression while in the shower to alleviate some of this discomfort. To hand express place your index finger and thumb on the outside of the areola at the 3'o clock and 9' o clock position. Push straight back and then roll forward. Repeat till milk flows.

*** Special Note: Ice is recommended to bring down swelling. Heat is ONLY recommended to eliminate discomfort if milk is adequately flowing or leaking from the breast. If you add heat to a breast where milk is NOT flowing, it can cause the tissue to swell even more. Ice first, moist Epsom salt hot soaks after.

- Cold compresses in between feedings (twenty minutes on, twenty minutes off) will aid in reducing swelling and relieving pain.
- Severe engorgement needs serious attention every feeding until it is improved. If left untreated, your milk supply may drop or subside altogether. Allowing the milk to sit in your breasts can lead to plugged ducts and or mastitis, a bacterial infection of the breasts.
- You may have read or been told to place green cabbage leaves on your breast. I would be very cautious when applying cabbage. The enzyme in the leaves absorbs into the breast and shrinks down the ducts. Super helpful when you are trying to wean, but in the beginning of the milk making process this can cause more damage than good.

If you are choosing not to breastfeed, your breasts don't know that and will produce milk anyway. Talk to a licensed lactation consultant about the steps needed at that point to dry up your milk supply.

3. CLOGGED MILK DUCTS / MILK BLEBS

Most lactating women will experience a clogged duct at some point, which, essentially, is caused by cheese, as weird as that sounds.

Plugged or clogged milk ducts happen when one of the milk ducts, or a localized area in the breast, becomes blocked, causing an obstructed flow of milk. Symptoms include tenderness in a localized area accompanied by a firm lump. The area usually is hot to the touch and swollen, with possible redness. Plugged or clogged milk ducts do not cause a fever, tend to come on gradually, and usually only affect one breast. The clog may appear at the very tip of your nipple, in which case it is known as a "milk bleb" (a clogged nipple pore), or the clog could be further back in the ductile system. Either way, it hurts. Some mothers may notice that the lump feels more painful before feeding, tender during"letdown, and less severe post feed.

Plugged ducts can be caused by:
- Inability to adequately empty the breast
- Lip or tongue tie in infant, making it difficult to empty the breast

- Engorgement
- Skipped feedings
- Inflammation due to breast infection or candida (yeast)
- Continuous added pressure on a specific duct, restricting complete milk flow (this is the most common reason). This can be caused by wearing a tight underwire bra, constantly holding the breast with your hand and fingers while feeding, or from placing a finger between the breast and the infant's nose. (Babies are obligatory nose breathers. If your baby can't breathe, she will come flying off the breast. No need to put yourself at risk of a clogged duct.)
- In some rare cases, reoccurring clogged ducts can be due to a retained placenta

The type of breast tissue you have plays a role in how prone you are to developing clogs. The more fibrous the tissue, the more clogs you may have.

So what do you do if you develop these pesky little plugs? First and foremost, keep breastfeeding! One of the best ways to remove the clog is to have your baby feed through it. Be sure to get plenty of rest and drink tons of fluids! The more you increase your fluids, the better your chances are for moving that clog out. If a clog is left untreated, it can lead to mastitis, a breast infection that requires medical attention, or a galactocele, which is a milk cyst that needs to be drained.

Here are some recommended steps to help you.

    A. Just prior to feeding, apply moist heat to the affected area either with a moist warm towel or by taking a shower. Must be moist heat; dry will inflame it.

    B. Soak the breast in a bowl of warm water and 2 tablespoons of Epsom salts for ten minutes prior to feeding. This is easier said than done, depending on where the clog is. If it is in an impossible location, then you can skip this step and just wrap in a hot towel.

    C. If you have a "bleb," or clogged nipple pore, then after soaking the breast in warm water, take a cotton ball saturated with olive oil and apply to the tip of the nipple. Let the oil soak in for about ten minutes, until dry. This will soften the skin and cover the bleb, making it easier for the clog to release.

    D. Soak the nipple using a Haaka (a silicone breast pump that uses suction) filled with Epsom salts and hot water. Suction it on and let it soak for ten minutes. It is very possible that you will see the clog loosen and enter the water. It legit looks like string cheese just came out of your nipple. (My daughter saw this happen in my clinic… best birth control ever.) NEVER use a needle to try and unclog the bleb. This can lead to increased damage and risk of infection. (I can't tell you how often I see this happen, and it make me cringe every time. If it is that deep then a doctor needs to attend to it)

E. Massage the area *before* and *during* the feeding. Stroke the breast in a downward motion from chest towards the nipple during the feeding. Using vibration can be very helpful as well. An electric toothbrush, a small vibrator, or a purchased breast massager that heats up and vibrates will work. (Seriously, gals, any vibrator will do. Who knew they could be dual purpose?)

F. Frequent feedings ensuring adequate emptying of the breast. It is really important to remove as much milk as possible from the affected breast.

G. Start feeding on the affected side, and if possible nurse a few minutes longer.

H. Avoid adding constant pressure with your finger or hand as mentioned above.

I. Position the baby so that her lower jaw is in alignment with the clogged duct. The baby's chin should be facing toward the plugged duct to allow the suction to be maximized toward the blocked area. Change positions to allow for adequate drainage of all ducts.

J. Have someone massage you between the shoulder blades to help aid in relaxation, resulting in better milk flow. The Du acupressure point works on adults as well.

K. As mentioned above: Take care of you! Drink plenty of fluids, rest, and, if possible, decrease your stress levels…which I know is easier said than done. You just had a baby, for goodness sake.

L. Avoid tight restrictive clothing and bras, especially with underwire.

SPECIAL NOTE If the clogged duct does not go away and you begin to develop flu-like symptoms, including chills and fever, call your doctor. You could be developing a breast infection known as mastitis.

If you have recurring plugged ducts, you may need to change your diet. Sometimes what we ingest makes our milk too thick and sticky. The following steps can help resolve recurring plugged ducts:

- Change your fat intake so you are only eating polyunsaturated fats.
- Moderate your salt.
- Add sunflower lecithin to your diet. This is an over-the-counter food supplement that works by decreasing the viscosity or stickiness of the milk. To prevent clogs, take 1200 mg daily. If you have a clog, see the lecithin treatment plan below. The brand

Legendairy Milk has a fantastic product (www.legendairymilk.com).

*** Make sure you are taking sunflower and not soy lecithin capsules. If you have a history of depression, take caution with soy lecithin, since soy is a phytoestrogen and can increase your chances of developing postpartum depression symptoms.

LECITHIN SIX-WEEK TREATMENT PLAN

Week 1–2: 3600–4800mg a day (1200mg capsules: 2 capsules, 2 times a day with food)

Week 3–4: 1 capsule, 2 times a day with food

Week 5–6: 1 capsule in the morning with breakfast

(May need to continue 1–2 capsules a day if stopping leads to additional plugged ducts

4. MASTITIS

Mastitis is a breast infection caused by an inflammation of the mammary gland due to milk not completely emptying from the breast. Bacteria can enter through cracked nipples, causing the infection to grow within the ductile system. Most women assume that if you have a breast infection, you can't breastfeed from the affected breast and that is NOT true! It is VERY important that you DO nurse from the infected breast. The milk will not be bad for your baby, and it is perfectly safe to feed. If you don't empty the breast completely, you risk further infection, or worse, a breast abscess, and trust me, you DON'T want that! That requires a surgeon to drain. So how do you know if you have a breast infection? Girl, you will feel like you have been hit by a Mack truck! It is quite painful. Other symptoms you may experience are:

- Flu-like symptoms: body aches, nausea, chills
- Fever of 101 or higher
- Red spots or patches anywhere on the breast. (BE SURE TO LOOK UNDER YOUR BREAST! That is a very common location for mastitis to be and can be missed. If you aren't feeling well, check it out!)
- A hard sore lump that is tender to the touch
- Breasts seem hot to the touch and are swollen
- Red streaks on the breast from the areola to the underarm
- Pus or blood in the milk
- Severe cracked nipples that are beginning to look infected with visible pus able to be expressed

If you notice any of these warning signs, there are two routes you can go. If you have a fever and feel like an abscess may be forming, the most important thing to do besides continuing to nurse is to schedule an appointment with your physician. You will need to be treated with antibiotics. The antibiotic that works best for breast infections such as mastitis is dicloxacillin, but there may be a better option specifically for your body.

If your doctor has diagnosed you with mastitis and has prescribed an antibiotic, be sure to take the medication as directed, completing the entire ten-to-fourteen-day course. If pain is inhibiting milk from letting down, place a warm compress on the infected breast to alleviate swelling while nursing on the healthy breast. After the swelling has decreased, breastfeed from the affected breast.

If caught early, there are some natural holistic options, such as homeopathy you can try prior to jumping into antibiotics. In my office, I have an ultrasonic wand with infrared light that I use to massage the affected area. The heat and ultrasonic waves actually help to reduce inflammation and literally melt the "cheese" so that the infected pus can be expelled. I know it sounds super gross, but it can be rather effective. I also recommend 1000 mg of vitamin C daily, or application of DoTerra Citrus Bliss oil.

Below is an excerpt written by Dr. Melinda Fischer, doctor of homeopathy. These are some of the remedies that can aid in healing:

Note: Nursing mothers can take Silicea 6X cell salts daily (not homeopathic remedy), to prevent recurring mastitis.

I've starred the most common remedies and put them first. The remedies should work within a short amount of time. If the pain is not resolved within twenty-four hours, then it's time to call your doctor.

Belladonna: This remedy is used when there is a sudden onset of Mastitis with rapidly rising fever. This is not a remedy that takes days to manifest. The breast is hot to touch, engorged, swollen, congested—red, hot breast. Throbbing pain in the breasts. The pain is worse from jarring. The right side is often more affected. The breast may have red streaks like sun rays extending out from the nipple

Hepar sulph: The breasts are very prone to abscess. Extreme sensitivity to the least touch; mothers can't stand for the baby to nurse. Complaints are worse from cold and exposure to the least draft, and better from warmth. Person feels chilly. This is a good remedy when there just aren't a lot of distinguishing symptoms.

Phytolacca: This is the most common remedy for about half of mastitis and blocked duct cases. Breasts become lumpy, with hard knots or nodules. Sore, fissured nipples. Intense pain in the breast as soon as the baby takes hold of the nipple. The pain often extends to the underarm or it can radiate over the whole body. Affects more often the right breast.

If the others don't work:

Arnica: Use this remedy if the inflammation follows an injury to the breast. Patients feel sore, bruised, and achy. There is fear to have the part touched.

Bryonia: Flu-like symptoms with general chills and fever, stitching pains in the breast, and headache. The breast feels hard and stony with stitching, needle-like pains. Any movement aggravates the pain. Usually the breast are not red as in the belladonna example. The patient will be quite irritable. Very frequently the patient will experience dizziness or faintness on rising from bed. There is strong thirst and not infrequently constipation.

Croton tiglium: This remedy is for when the mother has excruciating pain in the nipple that extends straight through to the back (at the level of the shoulder) with each suck of the baby. The breasts are very inflamed, swollen, and hard. The nipples may crack.

Lac-canium: Hypersensitivity to even the slightest touch of clothing on the breasts; jarring also aggravates.

Mercurius: Fever, chills, and perspiration without relief; the patient alternates between hot and cold, uncovering and covering.

For dosing, start with 30C, two to three times a day, until improvement sets in; then observe progress without taking further remedy as long as improvement continues. Repeat the remedy for apparent relapse. If the 30C potency of a given remedy acts well, but later ceases to help and the symptoms remain similar to previously, go up in potency to 200C. Do NOT take more than one day of repeated doses of a 200C remedy without professional help. Again, if this isn't resolved in twenty-four hours, it's probably time to get medical help.

**Caution – I have seen many articles by well-meaning though not professional people referencing the use of homeopathic sulfur for mastitis, and I just want to comment that sulfur is deep and long acting and really should be used with professional help.

Essential oils are also helpful when you experience cracked nipples. Of course, the cause for the cracked nipples should always be addressed as well (often, a bad latch is to blame). Just put a teaspoon or so of olive oil in your palm and add a drop of lavender essential oil. Rub palms together to mix and add a little warmth, and apply to nipple area after a feeding. If essential oils are more of your thing, here is an effective blend:

<u>Mastitis Blend</u>
10 drops melaleuca
10 drops lavender
5 drops Roman chamomile
Mix with 2 tablespoons of fractionated coconut oil
Massage from armpits toward the nipple area

5. THRUSH

Yeast infections are miserable. This pesky fungal infection can cause irritation almost everywhere in your body, and once you get it, it is very difficult to get rid of. These fungal spores set up shop wherever there are areas of moisture. Although most commonly found in the vaginal canal, now that you're breastfeeding, the breast, nipple, and areola are perfect breeding grounds. More often than not, the

81

infection is well under way before a diagnosis is even made. The longer it spreads, the more the fungus can wreak havoc on both you and your baby.

Yeast, formally known as candida, is the most common fungal infection in humans. Mammary candida is a yeast infection of the breast. Thrush is a yeast infection that is located in the mouth. Generally both mom and baby get infected and continuously spread the fungus back and forth to each other. It is recommended that both mother and baby be treated simultaneously in order to fully kill the infection.

To properly diagnose thrush, both mother and infant should be seen by their primary care physician. Candida is not very common on the breast and is often over diagnosed. Throughout the years I have seen so many doctors immediately prescribe fluconazole or nystatin at the mere sight of an irritated pink nipple. Can it happen? Of course, but usually only if baby has oral thrush, mom has a weakened immune system, or mom is prone to yeast infections. A culture of the breast would give an accurate diagnosis, but many doctors are unwilling to do that. Since the treatment is fairly harmless, doctors feel it is ideal to treat regardless.

Diagnosis is made from signs, symptoms, and clinical suspicion of the doctor. If mother has been diagnosed and baby has yet to, it is still recommended for both to be treated and vice versa.

Some predisposing factors to mammary candida are:

- Baby who has been diagnosed with thrush or fungal diaper rash
  - Previous history of vaginal yeast infections
  - Recent antibiotic therapy
  - Nipple damage
  - Heavy consumption of dairy products, heavily sweetened foods, and/or artificial sweeteners
  - Recent use of corticosteroid therapy

Symptoms of yeast in the baby include:

- White patches on the gums, cheek, or tongue. A white coating on the tongue does not automatically mean thrush. Milk tongue is white protein on the top of the tongue that is present because the baby is not able to lift the tongue to the palate to clean. Milk tongue you can usually wipe off. Thrush is raised, appears "hairy," and cannot be removed or scraped off. A pediatrician should be called to officially diagnose.
- Persistent frequent gas
- Red diaper rash, with raised pimple-like bumps that do not clear up with standard diaper rash ointment
- Frequently irritable infant who is continuously coming on and off the breast during a feed. Yeast hurts. It is itchy and burns, so feeding is very frustrating for these little ones. Can you imagine trying to eat while your mouth is constantly itching? Yikes!

- White discharge under the neck, armpits, and creases of skin that often smells like old cheese

Symptoms of yeast in the mother include:
- Burning sensation on the nipple during or after a feeding
- Sharp, shooting pains in the breast during or after a feeding
- Bright pink or red nipples
- Shiny red areola
- Small shiny abrasions at the base of the nipple that look like paper cuts
- Some cases have white discharge at the base of the nipple

As with most conditions of the breast, there are holistic and medical treatments. Yeast is tough to get rid of, so it may be that several remedies should be tried, especially if there are different strands suspected.

Medical steps for treatment of a yeast infection on the breast:
- Continue to breastfeed your baby; no interruption is necessary
- Referral to obstetrician, family practitioner, or pediatrician for official diagnosis

- Oral Diflucan (fluconazole) should be prescribed to treat the systematic yeast within the ductile system. (200–400mg STAT, then decrease to 100–200mg daily for fourteen to twenty-one days)
- Topical antifungal ointment such as miconazole, Gyne-Lotrimin, or AF Fungal cream should be liberally placed on the nipple and areola after each feed. Be sure to wipe the ointment off the breast with a warm wet washcloth before feeding the baby. Once the baby has been fed, reapply the fungal cream. If you are using nystatin cream in place of the above-listed ointments, it is not necessary to wipe the ointment off prior to feeding. The baby will most likely be treated with the same ointment, and it is perfectly safe.
- If baby is being treated with oral nystatin, be sure to shake the bottle first to thoroughly mix before using
- Use a gauze pad or Q-tip with warm water to gently wipe the baby's mouth after each feeding and then follow with the prescribed medication.
- Gently wipe nipple and areola with warm water after each feeding prior to reapplying the prescribed medicated ointment.
- Once treatment has begun, you should begin to feel relief in twenty-four to forty-eight hours, though in some cases, it may take three to five days or longer before relief is felt. Be sure to take the medication for

the full course, since the thrush may recur if you stop the medication simply because symptoms begin to disappear.

- Pain medication may be helpful, such as ibuprofen (400mg–600mg, depending on weight) every four to six hours as needed for breast pain. Anti-inflammatory medication should be taken with food. Consult your health care provider for proper dosing.

- Begin taking probiotics. Take one to two capsules of Mega Acidophilus within one hour after a meal (1.5 billion live cells per capsule, milk-free, hypoallergenic, no sugar, starch, artificial colors or flavors, no corn, wheat, soy or dairy).

- Baby should also be taking probiotics daily. Make sure you consult with your pediatrician on which brand is best. Yeast can often make your little one fussier and gassier, and she may demand shorter, more frequent feedings. Look for babies cues throughout treatment.

- While mother and baby are being treated for a yeast/candida infection, freshly expressed breast milk or refrigerated milk can be fed to the baby in the absence of the mother, with no problem. However, milk that has been expressed and stored during the outbreak of yeast should NOT be given to the baby on a later date as the fungal spores could reinfect the baby. Only when treatment is ongoing can infected milk be provided without any problems.

- Please keep in mind that it is very important to continue treatment for one to two weeks after thrush/candida symptoms have subsided in order to fully kill all infection

Holistic treatment:

- Consider limiting your sugar intake and restricting alcohol, cheese, wheat, and flour products
- Begin eating plain, unsweetened yogurt (Yoplait doesn't help. There is so much sugar added to flavored yogurts that it often counteracts the acidophilus properties)
- Open a probiotic capsule and mix with coconut oil. Apply on the nipple after each feed.
- Continue taking prenatal vitamins daily. Check to make sure your diet is not deficient in zinc, copper, vitamin A or B.
- Add garlic into your diet, which may boost the immune system and keep the yeast in check
- Avoid constant moisture on your nipples and areola. If you constantly leak breast milk, consider wearing cotton pads rather than plastic lined breast pads. DO NOT WEAR PLASTIC SHELLS.
- Sunlight and yeast are mortal enemies! Sunbathe your nipples for ten minutes, twice a day.

Expose all undergarments and breastfeeding equipment with direct contact to the breasts to sunlight.

- Add 1 tablespoon of vinegar to 1 cup of tepid water and apply to nipples and areola with a clean cotton ball after each feeding to prevent fungal growth
- Avoid restrictive clothing or underwire bras
- Boil all pump parts, pacifiers, bottle nipples, nipple shields, and toys with direct contact to the mouth daily for twenty minutes until yeast is gone. Place in the sun to dry.
- Discard and replace pacifiers and bottle nipples each week if needed
- Wash hands well to prevent further spread of the infection
- Increase rest, decrease stress….(I know this is sometimes easier said than done!)
- Wash all clothing, towels, and undergarments that come in contact with yeast in HOT water.
- Rub grape-seed extract on the nipples to reduce infection
- Gentian Violet is very effective, and relieves pain quickly, but is an outdated treatment. It stains your nipples and the baby's mouth purple and is very messy. Most mothers experience better relief from the previous treatments, and forgo the gentian violet. I personally love the color purple and thought it was

awesome to have purple boobies, but to each their own.

If symptoms persist, contact your health care provider and lactation consultant for further evaluation. There may be an underlying condition causing yeast-like symptoms.

6. VASOSPASMS/RAYNAUD'S PHENOMENON

Now we come to the ever-so-confusing vasospasm. Vasospasm is the sudden contraction of the muscular wall within an artery or blood vessel, causing constriction of blood flow. Basically it is as if your nipple fell asleep. Remember when you were a kid and you sat on your foot funky, and it would go numb? Then when the blood came rushing back, it hurt like a son of a gun? That is the same sensation, except it is your nipple. We can all repeat together...owie! Some vasospasms are caused by nipple clamping or compressions (often from a shallow latch or tongue tie), lack of magnesium resulting in poor circulation, or an underlying autoimmune disorder known as Raynaud's.

Raynaud's phenomenon can be very confusing. It can come and go, and the symptoms often mimic thrush. Symptoms can include:

- Shooting pains in the breast during and after a feed
- Burning nipples during and after a feed (sound familiar?)
- Blanched nipple after feeding or pumping (literally your nipple turns white, then purple, then pink)
- Relief with heat and compressions

- Same pain is felt with temperature changes
- Cold hands and feet. Feeling like you have to wear socks 24/7.
- Frequent headaches

Syndromes are tricky beasts that can come and go. However, there are some direct tricks that you can do to decrease the pain of a vasospasm.

- Visit an IBCLC to determine if there is a hidden tongue tie or shallow latch causing a crease or a lack of blood flow to the nipple
- Limit the intake of caffeine, as this can cause too much vasoconstriction
- Apply direct heat to the nipple right after you de-latch or pump. The sooner you can restore blood flow to the area, the better it feels.
- Take a supplement containing calcium 2000mg and magnesium 1000mg. (It is always recommended to consult with your doctor before adding any additional supplements). Calcium and magnesium are best friends and work best together. Magnesium can increase bowel movements, so if it gives you diarrhea, scale back on the dose.
- Take 500 mg of evening primrose oil
- Some patients take nifedipine, which is a cardiac vasodilator, but this should only be used in extreme situations and while under the supervision of a cardiologist

7. BACTERIAL INFECTIONS: STAPH OR STREP AND RED SKIN DISEASE

This sounds way scarier than it actually is, but it sure can hurt. It is not uncommon for us to have *Staphylococcus aureus* hanging out on our skin. Many women also carry the strep B bacteria. This can cause red, inflamed nipples and areolas. If there are cracks in the skin around the base of the nipple, it can absorb into the breast, which can then lead to mastitis. Often, doctors will blindly prescribe APNO (all-purpose nipple ointment), which consists of a topical antibiotic like mupirocin 2%, some form of an antifungal such as miconazole, and a topical steroid of betamethasone 0.1%. Basically, it covers all the bases. The problem with this is that doctors at times forget to tell the mom that she can only use this for ten days max. Some mommas love the relief of it and end up constantly smothering the concoction all over the breast and nipple. This can backfire and actually cause a breakdown in the skin, making it more susceptible to a topical bacterial infection known as red skin disease.

If you suspect that this is an issue, or your nipples feel like they are constantly screaming "This Girl Is On Fire," then push to have your doctor swab your breast and nipple area. There is absolutely nothing wrong with finding out specifically what it is you are dealing with. Some docs will fight you on that, but the antibiotics that work on staph and strep are very specific, so you have to be your own advocate.

Once you know what is going on, you can begin to treat those pesky bacteria correctly. (Side note: Some doctors will also prescribe lidocaine spray. I would advise against that. This is a temporary fix to a bigger problem. It may temporarily numb the nipple area, but it will also numb the baby's mouth, which is not good.) With most of these topical treatments, I would recommend wiping off the ointment prior to feeding. Baby will absolutely appreciate it.

8. PUMP TRAUMA

No one likes pumping. The machine can be uncomfy and the process is time consuming. And if you have the wrong flange, or have not been taught how to properly fit and use your pump, there is a possibility that you will end up with some raw, achy, circular rashes on your aureolas. Here are some things you can do to prevent traumatizing your boobies:

A. Make sure you have the correct fitting flange. Believe it or not, there are flange fitters that can help you. You also can go online at www.legendairymilk.com and use their online measuring tool.

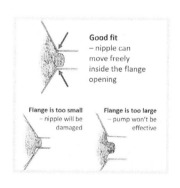

www.loveandbreastmilk.com

B. Lubricate the flange with coconut oil or olive oil. Repetitive pulling of a sensitive area through hard plastic is not pleasant. If you lubricate the flange, it will feel tremendously better and will cut down on the blisters.

C. If it hurts, turn down the suction. This is not the time to grin and bear the pain just to get a few extra drops. You will not yield more milk by having the bajeebies sucked out of your nipple. Make it comfortable. The strength should mimic the baby's suck. If you can see your nipple and areola being pulled to the very end of the flange, you are pumping too long, at too strong a suction, with the absolute wrong flange.

Once you find the right rhythm and method, if you still have pain, place some Soothie gel pads on and call your IBCLC. If you are in discomfort, it is very possible that so is the baby. There is no need to suffer through it. Breastfeeding is a learned art, but it doesn't have to be a Van Gogh. Find someone who understands your breastfeeding goals and is willing to think outside of the box, with a little creative encouragement.

Chapter 5: The Breastaurant

The number one question I get asked on the daily, if not hourly, is: How will I know if I am making enough milk for my baby? A breastfeeding mom's biggest fear is that her baby is going to starve and it will be her fault because she can't quantify the magical liquid in her boob. So to help rationalize this fear, she turns to Google... my nemesis! Please, for all that is holy, LET ME BE YOUR GOOGLE! Anything and everything is on the internet, both good and bad. Articles contradict each other. So you continue down the rabbit hole that is Facebook support groups, mom forums, Dr. Whatnots theory of everything, and before you know it, you have diagnosed yourself and your baby with pretty much every negative anomaly known within the crazy interweb. Ughhh!

With so many experts out there, and so many different philosophies, everything becomes extraordinarily complicated...and it doesn't have to be. It is JUST BREASTFEEDING, my dear beautiful mommas. As hard as it may be, try not to overcomplicate things. Find one person you trust, whose thought process encompasses your own beliefs, and come up with a solid plan together. If you put too many divas on a stage, they will all try to outshine each other,

94

and the one left in the shadows, sobbing, is you. Breathe, girl…I got you!

Allow me to break down the milk-making process for you. We already learned all about hormones and the anatomy of the breast. Now it is time to explain just how scientifically awesome your milk-making machines are. It is true what you hear about supply and demand. You have to remove milk to make milk. This is due to what we in the lactation world refer to this as FIL, or the Feedback Inhibitor of Lactation. Our pal FIL is a polypeptide, a whey protein, found in our breastmilk that controls the amount of milk production. The amount of milk made is based on how much milk the baby eats. You can't "fill up" till FIL moves out. If too much time goes by without milk removal, your body will actually slow down production, as the body takes that as a message that the faucets are ready to be turned off! Initially you will feel engorged, but if the milk stays static, it won't take long for your body to take the hint.

Your milk is made the minute that the baby sucks or the pump stimulates. The body will prepare, but the milk won't actually be made until stimulation occurs. It's like the supply truck comes to the breastaurant at 3 a.m. with all the ingredients it needs for the day, but no cooking is getting done.

And just like at a restaurant, different food is served at different times of the day. At 3 a.m. your prolactin hormone peaks so you will have more volume of milk in the morning.

At this time, more water will be drawn into the breast because the baby's need for hydration is higher. So you may make 4 ounces of breast milk at your breastaurant's "omelet bar," equaling twenty to twenty-six calories.

When the "lunch rush" happens in the afternoon, you have maybe one egg left, but if your little chef comes to the kitchen, she can still make something. At 3 p.m. your prolactin hormones are at their lowest, so you will have less volume. So she makes crème brûlée. At that feed you may only make 2 ounces, but it will have the exact same number of calories, 26, that the 4-ounce feed did, it is just richer, aka "crème brûlée." So if each feed is around 26 calories every time, the morning milk has 6.5 cal/ounce and 13 cal/ounce in the afternoon.

This is why it is so important to feed your baby on demand. Most babies cluster feed in the afternoon and early evening. If the baby is asking to go to the breastaurant more often on one day than the last day, then listen to their needs. You and I are hungrier on some days than others, and so are babies. Plus you never know when they are going through a growth spurt.

You will burn an extra 500–700 calories a day when breastfeeding, which is why some mommas lose weight when lactating. It isn't the most consistent weight-loss program, and not every women will lose weight, but it can certainly jump-start things. Talk about an awesome fitness plan! You get to eat constantly and rest with your cutie pie, all while burning calories. You will never feel hungrier and thirstier than you will when you are breastfeeding. In fact, feeling thirsty while nursing is a good sign that your hormones are working correctly!

I once heard a nurse say that babies are like little parasites, that they take all the nutrients we need to be strong and healthy. She was claiming that our children literally suck all that we need for ourselves from our milk. What a way to describe a baby! But she isn't wrong. Babies will take everything they need from us, and our bodies can suffer. That is why it is so important to continue taking your prenatal vitamins and to eat healthy. You will need around 75 grams of protein and around 2300 calories a day. That is A LOT of calories! That is like eating at In-N-Out four times a day. You will never reach that realistically, hence the weight loss, but the protein level is a must. (I just realized that some of you may never have heard of In-N-Out...it is basically the best fast-food burger joint EVER! Just think of burger, fries, milkshake.)

The one time your body will do a fight-or-flight is if you are not drinking enough water. Staying hydrated is crucial! You need to drink half your body weight in ounces. I know, I know...that seems like a lot and it is. However, if you are not staying hydrated, you will not make milk, period. Some of you may be having a difficult time remembering to drink water, or just do not like the flavor. *Body Armor* drinks are actually really great for increasing milk supply because of how well it helps you to hydrate. It is basically like a liquid IV. *Gatorade* has a ton of sugar in it, and that can cause other issues. It honestly doesn't help hydrate enough to counteract the amount of sugar.

The easiest way to remember to drink water is by drinking a glass every single time you breastfeed. That way you will at the very least get your eight glasses in! You will have to pee all the time, but your skin and milk supply will thank you.

It also is super important to remember the size of your baby's tummy and just how much they can handle. As their stomach grows, so will your milk supply. This visual should help:

Diagram : Medela

Day 1: tummy size 2–10ml per feed (0–24 hrs since birth)

Day 2: tummy size 5–15ml per feed (24–48 hrs)

Day 3: tummy size 15–30ml per feed (48–72 hrs)

Day 4: tummy size 30–60ml per feed (72–92 hrs)

Day 10: 60–90ml per feed

So let's bust through some of those myths that make you think you do not have enough milk for your baby. Remember, you cannot believe everything you hear on Google and Facebook.

Myth 1: My mom never made milk, so I won't either.

You are not your mother, sister, aunt, grandma, cousin Susie, or the random person you saw on Instagram. You cannot expect your journey to be the same as others when it comes to supply. Every mom is different and every baby is different. Even every pregnancy is different! I had tons of milk with my first daughter. I could feed the entire neighborhood if I wanted to. My second daughter…it felt like I had drops. It was literally half if not less than what I made with Alyssa. Same boobs, same mommy, different baby, different mouths. Your milk supply changes on the daily. It changes by the week. The volume will grow based on your baby's age and developmental needs. I know it is hard, but try not to compare yourself to anyone else. It doesn't matter if you are an overproducer or an under producer, just as long as you are a milk producer. There is a meme I just saw that said:

*Mom A produced 30 ounces a day, baby took 25 oz a day, therefore she is an **overproducer**.*
*Mom B produced 30 ounces a day, baby took 35 oz a day, therefore she is an **under producer.***

See the difference? Every woman will produce different amounts all the time, based on age of baby, weight of baby, and how much glandular tissue she has. If you are in fact not producing enough milk for your baby, then find an IBCLC trained in low milk supply. In my opinion, there is always a reason for low supply.

Myth 2: Foremilk hindmilk imbalance

This is a big one, as it is all over the internet and in every article you will ever read. And it is confusing as hell. But let me say this clearly—there really is no such thing as foremilk and hindmilk... there is milk and cream. I can hear the loud gasps from you all now. If you google "green poop," the first thing that will pop up as the cause is a foremilk imbalance. You will read that the baby is only getting the watery sugary part of the milk, sometimes referred to as lactose overload, not the part that is rich in calories, fat, and protein, resulting in green soapy-looking poops.

Remember how earlier I said that the milk is made the minute the baby sucks and that the milk is all made of the same constituents? (The morning milk has a higher ratio of water where afternoon milk has a higher ratio of fat and protein but it is all made from the same constituents.) When it sits, it separates. The fat and protein rise to the top and the water goes to the bottom. The morning milk just has a higher ratio of water where afternoon milk has a higher ratio of fat and protein, but it is all the same components.

If the baby did not happen to finish or empty the breast, the remaining milk will sit in the breast and separate. The fat and proteins will stick to the alveoli or milk ducts, and the watery

100

part of the milk will push to the front. Have you ever seen milk in a bottle separate, with the fat rising to the top and watery bluish milk sitting at the bottom? The same thing happens in the breast. For example: If your breast made 4 ounces at your 10 a.m. feed, but the baby only took 2 ounces from the breast, the remaining 2 ounces will then sit and most likely separate within the milk ducts. The next time the baby latches on, your body will again make the same 4 ounces. The 2 ounces that were left in the breast from the previous feed will then be pushed forward, with the newer milk coming in from behind. If you literally shake your breasts prior to feeding or pumping, the milk that has been static in the breast will mix together, making all the milk the same consistency. So before you feed, "shake the girls" and you will never have an imbalance again.

Now that isn't to say that there isn't the occasional mom who abnormally makes 10–15 ounces per breast (again, that is not common and should be evaluated for an underlying endocrine issue if this presents). There is no way a newborn is going to be able to take that amount of milk. In these cases, the baby can consume too much of the less-caloric "omelet bar" milk before reaching the newer fatty "crème brûlée" milk. These will result in slow weight gain and green soapy looking poop.

If the mother is not eating enough calories, protein, or fats in her diet, the same thing can happen. Her body will initially do fine, but the time will come when her body will suffer nutritionally, causing fewer calories or less fat to be formed in the milk. This, however, is extremely rare.

Myth 3: My pediatrician says that my baby was not back to birth weight by two weeks, so therefore I must not be making enough milk, or milk with enough calories, so I should supplement with formula.

Way to make a mom feel inadequate from the beginning. This is one of my biggest pet peeves. Birth weight is just a number, one that often is not accurate. The pediatrician and the hospital will keep track of your baby's weight after birth. If the baby has lost more than 10% of his birth weight by time of discharge, doctors often start to get concerned. What they aren't taking into consideration is the birth story. It is normal for the baby to lose 7–10% of weight in the first three days of life.

Birth plays a massive role in how you breastfeed. In fact, one of the first things I do when I meet a family is ask the mother to tell me her birth story. I want to hear her perspective of what happened. It often gives me a view into the big picture of how breastfeeding may go.

If mom has been induced or had an epidural, which 95% of mothers do, at least in California, there will be a false birth weight. The birthing staff will overhydrate you with multiple bags of IV fluids since the biggest side effect of an epidural is low blood pressure.

Overhydrating helps prevent this. But all of those fluids will also be pumped into the baby, therefore causing the baby to appear to weigh more than she actually does. Just like your ankles and face get puffy after being over hydrated, so does the baby. Her true birth weight is often what the discharge weight was on day three of life.

Now, if mom had an unmedicated birth, with no IV fluids, and the baby has lost more than 10% of his birth weight, then I would look at the output. Is the baby peeing and pooping? Babe should be peeing six times a day and having three yellow poops by the time they are one week old. If this is not happening, and the baby appears to be lethargic, sleepy at the breast, and has dry lips and concentrated urine, then it is time to supplement with your expressed milk or formula.

Remember that the calories and content of breastmilk changes throughout the day. Just like how you and I want to eat at certain points of the day more than other times of the day, your baby does also. As long as you follow your baby's cues, your supply will follow.

The other thing that pediatricians do not take into consideration, simply because most do not have the training, is whether the slow weight gain is due to oral tethering? If the baby has a submucosal posterior tongue tie (which often gets missed), a lip tie, or buccal ties, that critter is going to burn through tons of calories. Think about it this way, if baby has a tethered mouth, she is working as hard as if she were sucking a milkshake through a straw with a hole in it, while running

103

on a treadmill. Little one without a doubt will burn more calories than she is taking in. Baby will pee and poop like a champ, but not gain weight. If the output in the diapers does not match the weight gain, find someone trained in ties to examine your baby's suck. Get multiple opinions, and trust your mom gut.

Myth 4: One of my boobs is bigger and produces far more than the other boob. This must mean baby is getting half the amount of milk.

It has been said that we all have a stud and a dud, or as I like to call it, Splash Mountain and Milk Duds. I have heard IBCLCs refer to this as your boob and the better boob to remove the negative connotation that you are inadequate in your milk-making ability. I love that! Our mind is a powerful thing when it comes to making milk.

Good news! You only need one boob to fully feed a baby. The second one is the bonus boob.

For whatever reason, God decided to make every nipple size and shape different, and each breast capable of making milk in a different capacity. This pregnancy, good old lefty may be the heavy lifter. Next time around, your body might switch it up and righty over there will be the show-off. It has no bearing on your milk supply whatsoever, and often is determined based on preference from the baby.

If the baby has torticollis and is uncomfortable eating in a certain direction, the breast that little one can create the better seal on will definitely produce more. There are things you can do to help balance out the slacker side. For example, you can start your feed on the side that makes the least amount of milk. The stronger suck response from the baby may result in a higher milk making output. You can also use essential oils like basil and fennel mixed with a carrier oil and rub that on the smaller side as well. Or apply the Haaka or pump the slower side for about ten minutes after a feed to add better, more-frequent stimulation. Remember, our good pal FIL has to be removed!

Myth 5: I am small chested, only a size-A cup. I will not make enough milk for my baby like the larger-breasted women.

This could not be further from the truth! For the first time ever, size does not matter! I have often seen women with small breasts produce double what larger-breasted women can. It has nothing to do with the outside appearance it has everything to do with the "broccoli" inside. You can have huge double Ds and have a low supply, and have AA cup and make 6 ounces in five minutes. All that matters is how the baby latches.

The one exception to this rule is women with IGT, also known as insufficient glandular tissue. These breasts appear tubular, almost banana shaped, with just a bulbous areola. If there is no "broccoli," there are no glands to work with, and unfortunately not much can be done about that. However, we absolutely will try everything we can to help you make the most milk possible. Each breast has a capacity. If the capacity is maxed out, then you just feed more often.

Myth 6: My breasts are suddenly floppy and soft, therefore my milk is gone.

Could you imagine walking around every day engorged and clogged? Yikes! That would be so unbelievably painful. Several weeks after breastfeeding has been established, your body adapts to the amount of milk that is needed for baby. The tissue relaxes. The breastaurant has finally figured out the lunch rush! If you have ovulated or started your period again, that can absolutely cause a dip in supply, but baby will be quite vocal about that change, and that is temporary. If you are concerned, go back to the basics:

1. Is my baby peeing at least six times a day and pooping at least once?
2. Can I hear audible swallowing?
3. Does my baby seem satisfied after eating?
4. Is baby gaining weight?

If all of those are happening, then, girl, take a breath. You are doing exactly what your body was created to do. As hard as it may be, put the scale away. Do not weigh the baby after every feed. You will drive yourself bonkers. Instead, gaze at your baby, watch for the cues he is giving you. Take a minute for yourself and step away from the Facebook groups and Instagram…unless it is my Instagram page, then have at it. My point is, try not to overthink it. Your body is capable and willing. Let her do her thing!

Chapter 6: Low Supply

Our previous chapter was a rather lovely segue into the complicated tale of low supply. In my opinion, there is always a reason why a mother experiences low supply. It is either a mom issue, a baby issue, or a hot combo of both. We have already busted through so many of those Google myths, but let's actually dive into the abyss of low supply and how to make it grow. If you can figure out the root cause, you can figure out how to fix it. It is important to have realistic expectations. Some women will never be big producers, and that is okay. Remember, you only need 2 ounces of breastmilk for that baby to get the full immune benefits. If, for whatever reason, your body is not producing the amount that baby needs, cut yourself some slack. Think of the rich liquid gold that you are making as the baby's living vitamins. Every single drop counts. You are making a life-changing, life-healing super fluid that is specific to your baby! That, my beautiful friend, is the work of a superhero. Only YOU can provide the specific antidote to your baby's biological needs, even if it is a few drops. That is pretty flippin' incredible!

New mothers often assume that if their baby wants to "suck" more after feeding at the breast or "acts hungry," this must mean that they do not have enough milk. The majority of the time, mother's have plenty of milk—the baby just has a desire to suck. However, the concern of not making enough milk for your baby is a common one.

First we need to determine whether or not you truly have low milk supply. The majority of the time, it isn't that the milk supply is low at all. It is simply that breastfeeding is a learned art, and you may need to adjust the frequency of feedings. Even if your breast capacity isn't as big as another woman, that doesn't mean that your baby will not get the same number of ounces per day. It may just mean that your little one requires more feedings.

There also is a difference between delayed onset of lactogenesis (or delayed onset of your milk coming in) and low supply. Remember, you have been producing colostrum since you were ten weeks pregnant, but your mature milk typically doesn't come in until three to ten days after birth. If you happen to be one of those women who have a delay in their mature milk coming in, it can be perceived as low supply. If your baby is ten days old and you are still unable to express anything but drops, that is a reason for concern. It is extremely rare for a woman to not be able to lactate at all, so if this is you, it would be worth seeing a specialist for a workup.

The most common reason for a delay in your milk coming in is a retained placenta. If even a microscopic fragment of the placenta has been left in utero, it can make your body

109

think it is still pregnant and delay the milk from coming in, or result in multiple clogged ducts. This will also cause an infection and often heavy bleeding postpartum. If you are still bleeding significantly well after six weeks postpartum, you most definitely need to be examined by your doctor.

Another reason for delayed milk is a rare condition known as a theca lutein cyst, which causes an increase in testosterone postpartum. The balance between testosterone and prolactin is complicated, and this can suppress lactation for several weeks. Eventually the cyst, which is located on the ovary, will dissolve and milk will come in. This can be incredibly frustrating, and often leads to the mother ending her breastfeeding journey early. Mother will know if this is a problem due to an increase in facial hair and acne, a deepened voice, and a decrease in breast size. If mom continues to stimulate, her supply will eventually come, it just takes time and patience.

BIRTH STORY

Your birth story can also play a significant role in your milk production. If you have a cesarean birth, you will most likely experience a delay in your milk transitioning to mature milk due to the change in hormone response. Typically, moms will see their milk change closer to the seven to ten day marker rather than the standard three days. We are starting to see some hospitals and doctors be understanding about the impact cesarean birth can have on mother-baby separation or interruption of immediate skin-too-skin contact. This is a huge accomplishment. If the baby is able to be on mother's chest for the remainder of the surgery, it does help block the cortisol receptors that may impede the hormonal initiation of milk production. Having the baby next to your skin in those first few hours and days can make all the difference in the world.

If mother experienced an induction with Pitocin, this can also impact milk supply. Pitocin is the synthetic form of oxytocin, and it is used to artificially stimulate contractions. This puts added pressure on the baby's head with each contraction, often causing tension in the jaw, which can make latching a bit more difficult.

As I've mentioned previously, sometimes what seems like low supply isn't actually low supply. If mother had a large fluid load in labor (e.g., if she had an epidural or IV for longer than six hours), this will result in excess fluids within the breast tissue. This can make a mother feel more engorged initially, and when they experience a significant drop or delay shortly after, they interpret this as a loss of milk. As mentioned earlier, your baby also can have excess water weight, which can result in a false birth weight, leading the pediatrician to think the baby isn't getting enough milk.

There are many things that are misconstrued as low supply. There are also many genuine reasons that milk supply drops. It is important to understand the difference.

You are going to hear me repeat this several times in this book, because:

1. It is important to hear over and over again
2. Mom brain...enough said

If your baby is gaining weight without supplementing with any other form of milk, is having at least six to eight wet diapers and three to four dirty diapers a day until eight weeks and then pooping once daily from then on, then you do not have a low milk supply. Yippee! Trust the output ladies!

Thankfully, most paper diapers now have an indication stripe on the diaper letting you know when the diaper is wet. Man...how convenient is that! Back in my day (geez, could I sound any older), we had to put our finger in the diaper to check if it was dirty. That indication line is genius! I bet you never thought a yellow stripe turning blue could be so comforting.

If you are using cloth diapers, a good wet diaper will have about 45ml or 3 tablespoons of fluid. The urine should be pale yellow and not have a strong odor. By day five of life, poop diapers should be yellow and seedy with no meconium present and be about the size of a quarter or more, around 2.5cm.

Remember, a 7–10% weight loss is normal for a newborn. A breastfed infant should regain their birth weight by ten to fourteen days of life. Once the mom's mature milk has come in, then the baby should be gaining about 4–7 ounces a week. The behavior of the baby post feed, the weight or sensation of your breasts, the frequency of feeding, the sensation of letdown, or how much you pump are not adequate ways of evaluating whether or not you have enough breast milk.

If you are not sure if your baby is gaining weight because you haven't had a weight check recently, then your best gauge would be off of the number of wet and dirty diapers. What comes in must come out! When in doubt, check it out. Most breastfeeding support groups have scales where you can weigh your baby before or after a feed, or if need be you can schedule an appointment with your pediatrician or IBCLC to have a weight check. Do NOT however buy an infant scale, or weigh yourself with and without baby, after each feed. Nope! We have covered that one my friend! You will only cause yourself unnecessary anxiety. Motherhood alone creates enough of that.

Below are some of the most common questions and comments I get regarding low milk supply. These **DO NOT** mean that you have a low milk supply.

1. **My baby wants to eat all the time! He must still be hungry.**

It is true that breastfed babies need to be fed more frequently than formula-fed babies. This is because breast milk, being perfect food for the baby's gut, digests in just one and a half to two hours. Thus it is always best to be a baby watcher rather than a clock watcher.

Your baby may need to feed more frequently for various reasons. It could be a position issue. Or a tongue tie might be causing the baby to burn more calories than he is taking in. Because the proteins in breast milk are designed for your baby, it is impossible to overfeed a breastfed baby. If the baby is positioned correctly, then baby is in control of how much milk to remove from the breast.

You can however overfeed a formula-fed baby. The protein in formula is different and harder for the baby to breakdown and digest. This is why they often go longer in between feeds. Their little bodies take longer to digest the bovine or soy protein in the formula, which can make them sleepier. Not necessarily a good thing. How you hold the bottle also makes a difference in how fast or slow the baby feeds.

It is also possible that your baby is going through a growth spurt. Babies often go through growth spurts at three weeks, six weeks, and nine weeks of life, as well as at three months, six months, and nine months…notice the pattern? When this is happening, the baby will need to feed more frequently. Go off of your baby's cues. He or she will tell you when it is time to feed again. Growth spurts generally last a few days to a week. Remember our old pal FIL? The milk removal will cause you to "FIL" back up.

When your baby is naturally increasing the length and frequency of these feedings, try not to offer supplements unless medically indicated. Your baby feeding more often will signal to your body to make more milk. The more the baby nurses or stimulates the breast, the more milk your body will make. If you don't allow this to happen, and give a bottle instead, your body will not receive the message and most likely your milk supply will drop rather than increase.

And remember, sometimes your baby just needs to suck. There is a lot of research out there about non-nutritive sucking. This is part of the baby's calming reflex. The mother can choose whether to allow the baby to nurse as a source of pacifying or to use a pacifier. Personally, I like pacifiers. When used the correct way, they can actually help develop the baby's suck reflex and strengthen the suck, specifically post frenectomy.

Another very common reason your baby wants to feed more frequently, specifically in the newborn days, is simply because the baby is used to being with you 24/7. Sometimes, we just want our mommy. Babies need to feel close to feel secure. This is why skin-to-skin contact and "wearing your baby" is so very important. Not to mention it does wonders for your supply! There is so much scientific evidence supporting that even smelling your baby's head can increase your oxytocin release, thus increasing supply.

2. My baby will take 2 ounces of formula or expressed milk in a bottle after I have fed, without any problems?

Babies often will take a bottle willingly after a full, satisfying feed at the breast if the bottle is being angled downward, and the baby is on his back. The majority of the time this is due to a swallowing reflex the baby has. When milk is being poured into the baby's mouth, they are obligated to swallow, which elicits a sucking reflex. The baby isn't "gulping" or "sucking down" formula, they HAVE to swallow to be able to breathe again. This of course confuses parents, making them think the fussiness or sucking cues have to be because the baby is still hungry, when most likely it is the exact opposite. This, of course, leads to more bottles, resulting in less breast stimulation, which will eventually lead to a lowered milk supply. Not to mention that the kid has now been overeating, which will lead to reflux and projectile vomiting. Ahhh, the ever-so-comforting smell of baby barf, every new mother's perfume. I swear spit-up is an initiation rite of parenting.

3. But my baby is fussy.

All babies are fussy at certain times of the day. It is part of their neurological development. However, babies do not cry just to cry, which is why I take issue with the diagnosis of "colic." Colic isn't a thing. It simply is a term that physicians provide when they have no idea what is wrong with the baby. Crying is how babies talk to us, and there is always a reason. Often, this happens late in the afternoon or early in the evening, lovingly known as the witching hour, which makes mothers feel like they have run through their "quota" of milk for the day. Remember the analogy I gave earlier? You may have less volume, but the calories are the same. It is just richer. If baby is fussy, especially after a feed, it most likely is gas related. If that kiddo is truly still hungry, they will let you know. If you have tried everything, including white noise—my magic wand—and they are still fussy, then offer the breast again. If you need a break, then offer a bottle, but it may simply be that your little one needs some extra snuggles.

4. **I am not seeing any milk when I pump.**

A baby can always empty a breast far better than a pump can. The way a baby suckles elicits a completely different hormone response then the pump. We love our babies; we don't love the machine milking us. This is not an indication that you do not have milk. There are many mothers who have very abundant milk supplies, but who are unable to get much

of it out with a pump. A lot has to do with how you are using the pump, and what type of pump you have. Flange size is a big culprit, and you should definitely be sized. More often than not, you need a smaller size. There are different pumps for different needs. Some are strictly for stimulation purposes for when the mother is

separated from her baby, where others are solely for expression. A trained lactation specialist can analyze the situation and help you make the choice that is best for you. Also, I strongly recommend that you put socks on your bottles when you pump so you can't see them filling. If you are staring at the pump, your breasts can and will get performance anxiety. Cover them up so you cannot see how much milk is coming out. Amazing how powerful our minds can be.

5. My breasts feel softer and I don't have that tingly letdown response?

Not every woman is going to feel her letdown and that is okay. That is not an indication that you don't have one or that your anatomy isn't working. Some women feel the pins and needles rush of milk (I have my theories on why that happens, none of which have been proven scientifically). Other women only know based on the suck and swallow motion of the baby.

The longer you breastfeed, the better adapted your breasts will be, and the more at ease the cellular tissue will be. They will relax and won't always feel heavy and engorged all the time. This is a normal sign that your breasts have adapted to the amount of breast milk your baby needs. Your milk composition and the amount of milk produced will change based on your baby's needs.

These common concerns are frequent in new mothers, but are not causes of low supply. Now let's get in to actual low supply, which is related to various situations.

PART 1 :REASONS FOR LOW SUPPLY

In my years of practice, I have discovered that breastfeeding often brings to light conditions we didn't even know we had. When a woman comes into my office for a consult, the first thing I do after hearing about her birth story is get a full medical history. I want to know every tiny detail, girl. I do not want to leave any page unturned, any "T" uncrossed. Things that may seem unimportant are often the most relative clues in unlocking the mystery. If I can get a glimpse into what your story is, it will guide me in deciphering which route to go in discovering the why.

Breast surgery or insufficient glandular tissue (IGT) is an issue we must pay attention to. IGT, also known as mammary hypoplasia, is something that a woman is born with. As she grows, the breast tissue does not fully develop. This is one of the biggest reasons women decide to get breast surgery.

You might not even know your breasts are underdeveloped until you become pregnant and have a child. During pregnancy, hypoplastic breasts may not change very much, and you may have one breast that is significantly smaller than

119

the other or that appears tube-like. Remember, you only need one breast to do the job, but this is often very frustrating for the mother. If you do not have the glandular tissue, the breast cannot produce, no matter what we do. This does not mean that you are a failure or broken. You can and will breastfeed, it just may mean more frequent feedings and with less output. If a mother has implants, it is so important to find out what the breasts looked like prior. This will give us a good idea what there is to work with.

I have no problem with implants or breast augmentation. I practice in Orange County, California—half my client base has implants. But how the surgery can affect breastfeeding, depending on how it was performed. I would prefer that the implant be placed behind the pectorals rather than on top of them. The most uncomfortable aspect is that there is less room when you have implants, so when your milk comes in, you may feel more engorged then the mother who does not have implants.

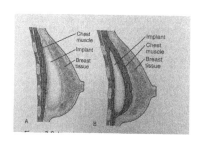

Figure A. Between breast and muscle. Figure B. Behind muscle. Walker, Marsha. *Influence of Maternal Anatomy* pg110

Caption

A peri-areola incision is the safest option, despite nerves being cut. Nerves can regenerate. If the surgery happened at least five years prior to breastfeeding, then the likelihood of that affecting the nerve pathway is slim. "Anchor" incisions carry a higher risk of causing supply issues, since there is a strong possibility that milk ducts were severed. Scar tissue can form and make it more difficult to express milk. Any interference with the pathways for the hormone release will naturally impact the breasts' ability to produce.

If the incision is under the armpit, I do not worry as much, though there is a risk that glandular tissue was severed. When this happens, the "broccoli flowerets" are separated from the "stem" so there is no place for the new milk to travel to. If the milk cannot be removed, then the supply will drop.

Breast reductions do pose a problem with milk supply, as more often than not, milk ducts are removed along with the breast tissue. I always recommend moms consult with their surgeon about their desire to breastfeed ahead of time to weigh the risks and the benefits.

We have to be out-of-the-box thinkers. Breastfeeding, motherhood, and especially supply, are not cookie-cutter processes. It is very individualized, and therefore must be treated as so. It often can vary from child to child as well.

Usually the biggest culprit for low supply is **hormones and anatomy**. I want to know if you had difficulty getting pregnant, if your breasts showed visible change in size and color, if you conceived naturally or needed the help of a fertility specialist. If you had to do IVF or IUI, I will ask if it was due to a health concern on the mother's side or a deficiency from the dad's side. This is super important. So many lactation professionals immediately assume that if a mother has had an IVF-assisted pregnancy, it was due to her hormones or physical anomalies. Sometimes it can be just as much the man as it is the woman. Understanding the hormonal history of both is crucial.

If the mother had no difficulty conceiving, had positive breast changes (the breasts got bigger and darker), then chances are that the low supply is not related to her lactation hormones. There are, however, many endocrine conditions that can predispose a mother to low supply such as hypothyroidism, polycystic ovarian syndrome (PCOS), diabetes and other insulin-dependent conditions, theca lutein cysts as we discussed earlier, hypoglycemia, and of course high levels of cortisol, our stress hormone.

Thyroid disorders are one of the biggest culprits of low supply and can be triggered by pregnancy. They can present as hypothyroidism, hyperthyroidism, or postpartum thyroiditis. They all have a significant effect on milk supply. I believe that every woman should have their thyroid checked six weeks postpartum as part of their routine blood work, especially if there is a family history of thyroid disorders. We have to take into consideration the enormous physical changes our body chemistry has just gone through, not to mention the epigenetic changes that are happening due to our environmental influences.

Hypothyroidism is when your thyroid (the butterfly-shaped gland in your neck) is not producing enough thyroid hormone, resulting in a slowdown of your metabolism. The thyroid hormone plays a significant part in regulating prolactin and oxytocin, the two main hormones of lactation. Symptoms can include excessive fatigue, hair loss, constipation, weight gain, and of course a decrease in milk. Low thyroid levels are associated with lower fat content of the milk, decreased milk production, low prolactin levels, and poor weight gain in the baby. The thyroid is responsible for cellular activity. If there is a slowdown in the milk-secreting cell activity, supply will continue to decrease.[3]

Polycystic Ovarian Syndrome, also known as PCOS, is a tricky beast. It is a complex combination of endocrine, ovarian, and metabolic dysfunction. It can manifest in many ways, including obesity, irregular periods, higher androgen levels, growth of dark body hair, and insulin resistance. About 10 % of women in their reproductive years will develop PCOS. Most women with this condition will not have a full supply with their first baby, but that does not mean that these mommas are doomed forever with their supply. Due to prolactin receptors, which increase with each pregnancy, they often produce more with subsequent births. Depending on the methods used, some women will be able to have a full supply.

Insulin plays a huge role in milk supply. In a new study by Dr. Nommsen-Rivers published in July of 2013 and later updated in 2018, she explains the genetic switch that happens during the first few weeks of breastfeeding.[4] During lactation, the human breast is extremely sensitive to insulin. The reason so many women have trouble with supply is partly because so many women are prediabetic and insulin dysregulation undermines their supply. Dr Nommsen-Rivers says: "This new study shows a dramatic switching on of the insulin receptor and its downstream signals during the breast's transition to a biofactory that manufactures massive amounts of proteins, fats and carbohydrates for nourishing the newborn baby. Considering that 20 percent of women between the ages of 20 and 44 are prediabetic, it's conceivable that up to 20 percent of new mothers in the United States are at risk for low milk supply due to insulin dysregulation."

This is why it is extremely important to pay attention to your protein intake and to exercise and stay hydrated. It is also key to consult with a trained IBCLC, as certain herbs like fenugreek can actually lower your blood sugar, causing a huge dip in supply. It would be catastrophic for a momma who is trying so hard to build her supply to have Google's most popular galactagogue tank it.

Stress and cortisol hormone are oxytocin's worst enemy. You could have every pump, every herb, every supplement in the world, but if you are under significant stress, your supply will tank. Now, I know what you are thinking…find me a mother with a new baby, and a partner that may or may not understand, that isn't stressed. You are solely responsible for raising this tiny person. Their growth and success rides on what you do. Meanwhile, you are not sleeping or showering, and you are attempting to work a full time job. Motherhood is extremely stressful!

One mother I worked with had no pre-existing reason to not make milk. This was her fourth baby, and she'd never had an issue with milk supply until now. She had no hormone imbalances, no previous breast surgery or health conditions. Her thyroid and insulin levels were normal, and we were stumped. Then it hit me. Her husband was in the military and was deployed. Her mother, who was a former IBCLC, had recently passed away. This was the first time she was breastfeeding a baby without the help of her mother or her partner. Between her stress and her grief, this sweet momma no longer believed that her body was capable. And her baby was sensing her grief and responding to it. No matter how hard she tried, she could not produce. After a very powerful venting session with me, she was able to release that stress, cry for the first time, and FEEL what she needed to let go of. And before you know it, the floodgates opened and she began leaking. It was such a powerful moment, one that I will carry with me forever. Stress is nasty and will wreak havoc on every facet of your life if you let it.

So what do you do about this one? Find your village! You are not alone in this. If you are feeling overwhelmed or stressed, find someone to give you breaks, someone you can vent too. There are so many wonderful resources out there now, even online, that can help you to find your purpose and get you on a path that feels safe and normal.

PART 2: How to Help Low Supply

Determining the possible culprit of your low production will help you figure out how to build your supply back up. With all of these treatments, I do still strongly recommend pumping, frequent feeding/milk removal, and meeting with an IBCLC to create a personal plan that works for both you and baby. I personally am not a fan of triple feeds, which is when a mother pumps immediately after breastfeeding and supplements with formula in a bottle. It can be very overwhelming for mothers. However, if you have found an IBCLC that you trust, allow them to guide you. Here are a few things you can do in the meantime:

GALACTOGOGUES

Galactagogues are herbs and other substances that support breast milk production and increase milk supply. Most of these herbs are available to you over the counter, but it is strongly recommended that you seek the advice and care of an IBCLC-licensed lactation consultant to help you choose the galactagogue that is best for you and your specific situation. For example, years ago, the most commonly used herb for increasing supply was fenugreek. I explained earlier how this can devastate a milk supply for a mom struggling with insulin resistance. I STRONGLY CAUTION YOU NOT TO USE THIS HERB!

Herbs That Can Increase Supply

Blessed Thistle (*Cnicus benedictus*) – This herb, native to Europe and Asia, has a calming effect on women and helps reduce anxiety, increasing a new mother's comfort level during what can sometimes be a frustrating and exhausting situation. This stimulates blood flow to the mammary glands, thus helping milk production.

Nettle (*Urtica dioica*) – This herb helps breastfeeding mothers by providing additional nutritional support that is sometimes lacking in the woman's diet. It has been documented to be a rich source of iron, calcium, and folic acid. This is however a diuretic and should be used carefully, as it can result in frequent loose stools.

Goat's Rue – Aids in developing additional mammary tissue for women who have PCOS, women who are adopting and inducing lactation, or women who have had breast reduction surgery. It may also have a positive effect on insulin sensitivity and is thought to be the precursor for the popular diabetes drug metformin.

Fennel (*Doeniculum vulgare*) – This herb travels to the baby through the breastmilk and has been known to stimulate feeding cues and aid in the infant's digestion, relieving colic and excess gas.

Ixbut – Used by the indigenous populations of Central America to stimulate milk production in humans and cattle for centuries. It is traditionally served as an herbal tea due to its light, nutty flavor.

Moringa – A nutritional powerhouse native to Asia that has been shown to increase milk production within just a few days of taking it. It's believed to work by boosting prolactin levels (the major milk-making hormone)

Shatavari – One of my favorites. Shatavari has its origins in India and is popular as a restorative tonic for various female health issues. It has been known to stimulate mammary gland growth and increase milk production. It has been compared to Reglan for treating gastric problems and it appears to cause a similar increase in prolactin without the awful depressive and neurological side effects that Reglan can cause. A wonderful option is shatavari/cardamom tea by Traditional Medicinals. Make sure you buy the shatavari blend with the green flowers on the package. Available at Sprouts, Amazon, Whole Foods.

Torbangun – Used as a traditional food to stimulate lactation for the month or so following childbirth. The plant is high in iron, potassium, calcium, and magnesium. Most commonly ingested in a tea form.

Alfalfa – A highly nutritious plant that is said to boost milk supply, stimulate mammary gland growth, and increase milk fat content. It can also promote vitality and improve water retention for mamas with postpartum edema. It can be taken both during pregnancy and after birth. **CAUTION: Do not use alfalfa if you have a peanut allergy or an auto-immune disorder such as lupus, as extra inflammation can occur.**

Anise – An aromatic seed traditionally used in Europe to help improve the flow of milk and soothe colic or gassiness in babies.

Black Seed – A rich source of fatty acids, protein, and minerals such as calcium and iron. It's known to stimulate the release of prolactin (the major milk-making hormone), promote mammary gland growth, and increase milk production.

Choosing the right combination of herbs can be tricky. It truly is a case-by-case judgment, which is why you should consult with a breastfeeding specialist. Most lactation consultants will evaluate the situation and then decide what level of treatment to begin with. It will often be a combination of herbs.

The best and safest selection of herbal blends can be found at www.legendairymilk.com. This is what I personally recommend to my patients. The founder not only makes fantastic products, but she is a low producer herself with PCOS. She is brilliant and her products are amazing.

Herbs That May Decrease Milk Supply

Large amounts of the following herbs and other natural remedies should be avoided while nursing because they have been known to **decrease** milk supply. The amount of these herbs normally used in cooking is unlikely to be of concern; it's mainly the larger amounts that might be used therapeutically that could pose a problem. However, some moms have noticed a decrease in supply after eating things like dressing with lots of sage, sage tea (often recommended when moms are weaning), lots of strong peppermint candies or menthol cough drops, or other foods/teas with large amounts of the particular herb. These herbs are sometimes used by nursing mothers to treat oversupply, or when weaning.

- Black Walnut
- Chickweed
- Herb Robert (*Geranium robertianum*)
- Lemon Balm
- Oregano
- Parsley (*Petroselinum crispum*)
- Peppermint (*Mentha piperita*)/Menthol
- Periwinkle Herb (*Vinca minor*)
- Sage (*Salvia officinalis*)
- Sorrel (*Rumex acetosa*)
- Spearmint
- Thyme
- Yarrow

ESSENTIAL OILS

Excerpt by April Kurtyka, IBCLC, Aromatherapist

The number one oil you want to use caution with while breastfeeding is peppermint. Some women don't see a huge drop in their milk supply when it is used, but many do. This includes ingesting peppermint as well as applying it topically or even diffusing it.

Now, let's move on to the fun stuff—how you can use essential oils while breastfeeding! First rule is that I don't suggest putting oils directly onto your nipples because this can cause nipple aversion for baby if they don't enjoy the taste or if the smell is just a little too strong. The only caveat is when you are treating cracked nipples, in which case you will want to gently wipe off your nipples before feeding.

Second rule I have is to always dilute your essential oils before using them. Why? Because they are powerful! Women's bodies often react differently during pregnancy, postpartum, and lactation then they do normally. I always prefer to err on the side of caution during these times because who wants to deal with a skin reaction when they are also dealing with something like cracked nipples, right?

Some of my favorite oils to use to increase milk supply are clary sage(which is VERY different than regular sage), fennel (do not use longer than ten days at a time), basil, and geranium. You can use any of these along with a carrier oil like fractionated coconut oil, almond oil, or olive oil.

More Milk Blend
2 drops fennel
4 drops of clary sage
add to 10ml roller bottle
fill to top with fractionated coconut oil
Apply to breast excluding nipple area after nursing (to encourage milk flow for next feeding)

ACUPUNCTURE
Excerpt written by Lauren Messelbeck, LaC

The human body response that most strongly affects lactation is STRESS. The human stress response is controlled by something called the autonomic or automatic nervous system, which can be broken down into the sympathetic nervous system—the gas pedal—and the parasympathetic nervous system—the brake.

The stress response is important in life-threatening situations, but when stress becomes chronic it leads to the most common life-threatening diseases in the United States. After the initial surge of epinephrine or adrenaline, our body goes into a second gear to keep the stress response going, relying on hormones such as cortisol. The physical effects of chronic stress/cortisol are:

1. Rapid breathing
2. Increase in blood pressure
3. Increase in blood sugar. Epinephrine triggers the release of glucose and fats from temporary storage sites. Over time this will make it difficult for people to lose weight.
4. Fluctuation in hormones. It is very common for stressful situations to lead to a reduction in the hormones that cause milk ejection.

5. Low libido. Oxytocin is released during sexual intercourse and allows for the proper milk ejection and letdown response.
6. Insomnia
7. Weakened immune system. Becoming sick is a common reason for reduction in milk production. I see this commonly with the second baby and mama's with preschool age children at home. The medications to treat cold and allergies can also affect milk production.
8. Increase in depression. Multiple studies indicate that postpartum depression (PPD) **interferes with breastfeeding**. Postpartum women who suffer from depression are less likely to breastfeed, and they typically breastfeed for a shorter duration than women who are not depressed.
9. Tense muscles. The proper ejection of milk is controlled by the proper contraction of the muscles surrounding the glands responsible for milk production.

Now it is important to understand how acupuncture affects the stress response in our bodies:

1. Evidence suggests that acupuncture decreases sympathetic activity and increases parasympathetic activity

2. Evidence shows that acupuncture enhances the activity of endogenous opioid peptides, serotonin, dopamine, and GABA, all substances that help stabilize our mood, enhance sleep, and decrease overall inflammation in the body

Acupuncture also improves blood flow throughout the entire body, with vasodilation both at site of application and at a distance. A common question I get from patients coming in for acupuncture for lactation issues is where I am going to put the needles. They imagine me poking their tired and overused boobies.

Acupuncture has been shown to specifically help with lactation issues. A randomized-controlled trial in Sweden on acupuncture for the relief of inflammatory symptoms of the breast during lactation concluded that women who received acupuncture were less likely to develop an abscess, had less severe symptoms on day five, and had a lower rate of fever than women in the usual care group.[5]

Another study, published in 2019 in the journal *Medicine*, found acupuncture and tai na (massage) to be successful in treating postpartum women who underwent a C-section with insufficient lactation.[6] The acupuncture group had significantly increased milk production when compared to the control group, by as much as 13-fold.

Research conducted at the Hanzhong Shanxi Hospital demonstrates that the application of a specific set of acupuncture points significantly boosts lactation quantities.[7] In a controlled investigation of 116 women with low milk supply, acupuncture successfully increased breast milk secretion from an average of 49.63 ml to 115.21 ml, in a matter of days. In addition, lactating mothers receiving acupuncture had a significant increase in their prolactin hormone.

Women often ask me for acupuncture points they can stimulate on their own to increase or regulate milk production.

Acupressure to the points explained here is a great way to stimulate production outside of any acupuncture treatments. Stimulate with pressure and a gentle clockwise motion on/ around the points for fifteen to thirty seconds. The best times to practice your acupressure include:

- When pumping
- When nursing
- In the shower
- While brushing your teeth
- During nap time
- Before feedings

Acupressure Points for Insufficient Lactation

(All acupuncture points are named for the internal organs that the channel connects to. Recommending a point on the liver or small intestine channel does not indicate pathology of your internal organs.)

Small Intestine 1

Location: On the outside of the last joint of the little finger. At the corner of the nail.

Indications:

- Insufficient lactation, acute mastitis
- Sore throat, conjunctivitis, headache

SI 1 is the empirical point for insufficient lactation. A study in a Chinese hospital explored the specific effect of acupuncture at Shaoze (SI 1) for treatment of postpartum hypolactation.[8] Two hundred and seventy-six cases were divided into a treatment group and a control group, half in each group. The treatment group was treated with electroacupuncture (EA) at Shaoze (SI 1) and the control group with EA at Shangyang (LI 1). After treatment of just two courses of acupuncture, milk production was increased 97.8% in the treatment group and only 24.3% in the control group.

The treatment group also had an improvement in mammary filling (the time it takes for the breast or mammary glands to begin to refill), an increase in the amount of milk, and improved prolactin levels.

Stomach 18

Location: On the chest, directly below the nipple, at the base of the breast, between the fifth and six ribs.

Indications:

- Acute mastitis, insufficient lactation
- Chest pain, cough, and asthma

I will also have patients experiencing depression (there is a lot of that after having a baby, even just a grieving of your past life before this baby came into your life) apply pressure to a point just below this one, between the sixth and seventh rib (LV14), which is great at moving blood and energy in the chest and relieving stress.

Ren17

Location: Translated as chest center, this point is found at the center of the breast bone in line with the fourth rib, between the nipples. Breasts can vary in location on the chest, so line it up with where the bottom of your breast protrudes from the chest wall.

Indications:

Regulates energy in the chest, important point for breast disorders and promoting lactation.

KD25

Location: This point lies over the mammary lymph nodes. On the chest, in the second intercostal space (between ribs two and three), two inches to the outside of the center of the body.

Indications:

• Cough, asthma, chest pain

• This point is a reservoir of nourishment specifically for the spirit. It is a deep spiritual spring, a reserve on which to call in hard times, when the patient has very little on which to draw.

ST36

Location: This point is located four finger widths below the knee cap with the leg extended, on the outside of the tibia, which is the most prominent bone in your lower leg.

Indications:

This point is one of the most common points used in Traditional Chinese Medicine. It is the primary point to replenish and tonify energy, blood, and yin. It is commonly used in postpartum dizziness and is indicated to treat chest pain, swelling of the breast, and breast abscess. This one is also great at getting digestion regulated after giving birth.

Spleen 6

Location: On the inside of the lower leg, four fingers above the highest point of the ankle bone.

Indications:

Regulates menses, balances hormones, improves sleep, and calms the mind. This point is commonly used to treat problems with fertility and gynecological problems. It is also the meeting point of all the yin channels and useful for mothers with young children who are not sleeping through the night for prolonged periods.

MEDICATIONS

There are two medications that are known to help increase supply, but they should be used with caution. Ironically, both are GI/stomach medications used for nausea and delayed gastric emptying.

REGLAN: This is an FDA-approved medication in the United States for increasing breast milk. It stimulates the pituitary gland, thus causing more prolactin and more milk. Typically, your OB will prescribe a low dose and gradually increase as needed. It does, however, cause some neurological side effects and can increase anxiety and postpartum depression. I can personally attest to this. I was actually trying to wean while on Reglan for delayed gastric emptying. It did in fact increase my supply (which was not what I needed, as I was trying to dry up my supply), but I felt like my skin was crawling. It was an awful feeling. I became paranoid, anxious, and very cranky. As soon as I realized it was the medication, I stopped. I never recommend this as a treatment. There are many other alternatives that work far better. My advice is to always try natural therapy before medication, if possible.

DOMPERIDONE: This is another GI medication that has a side effect of increasing supply, but it is much safer than its cousin Reglan. Other names for this medication are Motillium and Vomitstop. This medication however is not FDA approved in the United States for increasing milk supply. We are the only country that chooses Reglan over domperidone. Most countries have banned Reglan for use as a galactagogue and only prescribe domperidone, which is why it is easier to obtain through an online pharmacy. I do recommend, however, that you discuss the risks and benefits with your doctor and IBCLC prior to taking any new medication.

Typically it works best for mothers with endocrine issues such as PCOS and mothers who are choosing to induce lactation. Typically, the starting dose is 10mg three times a day, but Dr. Thomas Hale, renowned pharmacist and expert in medications and mother's milk, has advised up to 90mg a day, even though there is no evidence to support which dose works best. A recent study published in the **Lactmed, NCBI journals** cautions that mothers with a history of cardiac arrhythmias should not receive domperidone, and all mothers should be advised to stop taking domperidone and seek immediate medical attention if they experience signs or symptoms of an abnormal heart rate or rhythm while taking domperidone, including dizziness, palpitations, syncope, or seizures.[9]

Regardless of which route you take to increase your milk supply, please take a full medical history into account, and do not be afraid to be your own advocate. Every ounce, every drop you produce is a gift for your baby. You got this!

Chapter 7: Oversupply and Overactive Letdown

It would seem that every breastfeeding mother would desire to have a milk production so big that you would have endless freezers full of expressed milk. Your baby would always be blissfully full and content, and your breastfeeding worries would be over. Surprisingly, this is not always the case. In fact some women actually suffer from an overabundant milk supply. Although that may seem like every lactating woman's dream, an overabundant milk supply can be rather bothersome.

Sometimes the flow is so strong that it makes it difficult for the baby to stay latched on. This can cause a fussy baby, more gas, and ultimately more spit up. The baby may come off the breast quickly or cough and "sputter" due to the spray of milk, which can be frightening to any new mommy. If the mother is constantly making large quantities of milk, she may be facing frustrating breast conditions such as frequent clogged ducts, mastitis, or painful engorgement. It can seem like a never-ending battle. Not only are your breasts constantly in pain and your shirt always soaked, which is unpleasant in itself, but it can be isolating as well. Just

143

because you're making enough milk to feed the entire neighborhood, that doesn't mean you will be supported by your motherhood community. Mom guilt comes with this condition as well. You feel bad for complaining that you make too much when there are others who cannot breastfeed at all. Motherhood is hard enough without isolating women based on their ability to make milk. We are stronger together.

There are many reasons why hyperlactation—aka mega milk maker—occurs. Initially, it may just be due to overstimulation and unnecessary use of galactagogues. Yet, as I see many times over, it could be a sign of a more serious condition.

Some of these would be :
- Neoplastic processes (prolactinoma)
- Hypothalamic pituitary disorders
- Cushing disease
- Thyroid malfunction, such as hyperthyroid or Hashimoto's

A simple blood test and, if needed, an ultrasound can tell if there is any abnormality.

Women with hyperlactation make excessive amounts of milk, such as 300 to 400ml (10 to 14 ounces) per session. On average, milk production within the first week ranges from 200 to 900ml (6 to 30 ounces) a day with a milk synthesis of about 11 to 58ml (.4 to 1.96 ounces) an hour. The breasts will eventually calibrate the amount of milk to make based on baby's intake. When a mother makes too much milk, the synthesis ends up being closer to 60ml (2 ounces) an hour or even higher.

If this sounds like you, here are some tips to help reduce the milk flow to a level that the infant can handle, as well as reduce your milk supply to match the needs of the baby.

- Try block feeding with one breast per feeding session. Waiting up to three hours between feedings may naturally decrease your supply by decreasing the demand. It is always recommended to feed your baby on demand, but instead of switching breasts, allow one side to empty before offering the other breast. If the baby wakes up and wants to return to the breast in less than an hour, offer the baby the same breast that was used at the previous feeding. If it has been over an hour, I would recommend switching to the other side. If your other breast (the side that the baby did not feed on) is uncomfortably full, you can pump it out, but I would not pump for longer than ten minutes, as this may send a mixed message to your brain to produce more. Remember, your breasts work by supply and demand. You want to pump long enough to empty for comfort, but not too long to tell your brain to make more. Five to ten minutes is appropriate.

- For a strong overactive letdown, try pumping or hand expressing for a few minutes just prior to the feeding to allow that first initial forceful spray to happen. This way it won't spray into the back of the baby's throat, which can make your baby bite down to help slow down the flow. That does not feel good! Pumping can usually be discontinued after one week as the supply begins to decrease slightly. Try to make a conscious effort to relax during the first milk-ejection reflex.

- Latch the baby and breastfeed in a more reclined position. Try lying down with the baby so that the baby is coming towards you, tummy to tummy. This will be going against gravity, resulting in a less forceful spray.

- Try other nursing positions with your baby's head higher than the rest of his body. If you choose to use the cradle hold, be sure to have good pillow support, and lean back. Or position the baby so that he is straddling your leg, directly facing the breast, with his head slightly above the nipple in a koala hold.

- Apply direct pressure with the base of your hand to the opposite breast you are feeding from, to help control the flow.

- If your baby begins to choke or gag because he received too much milk too fast, de-latch the baby gently from the breast, hold him upright, burp him, and calm him down. Hand express some milk till the spray has slowed, then resume nursing.

- Try not to let the opposite breast become engorged. Hand expression or pumping just enough to relieve some ductal pressure will help, but remember to avoid vigorous pumping. Pump only if it is necessary for comfort.

- It is important to watch for signs of mastitis. If you feel like you are coming down with the flu, experience sore, red breasts, headache, fever, body aches, and other flu-like symptoms, call your OB or other caregiver, as an antibiotic will be needed.

- Once your body has figured out how much milk to make, resume breastfeeding on both breasts at each feeding. Usually within a week, your milk supply should have regulated.

Drinking peppermint tea can also lower your supply, as can sage and parsley tea.

There is a difference between an overactive letdown and oversupply. On overactive letdown is when a mother can produce a normal amount of milk, but have a milk ejection reflex that is strong and overpowering. Oversupply as mentioned above does not necessarily mean you will have an over active letdown. However, these tips can be helpful for both circumstances.

If you have a true diagnosed over active letdown, e sure to shake the breasts prior to the feed and watch for signs of milk ratio imbalance (which again is rare) by looking for frothy lime green poops and very little weight gain. This would indicate that your body is not given the chance to loosen any of the fatty part of the milk that may be stuck within the cellular walls of the milk ducts, thus resulting in a lack of complete composition of milk provided to the baby.

If you continue to have overabundant supply after following these suggestions, consult with a Board Certified Lactation Consultant or your physician to see if there may be an underlying health condition causing an increase in supply.

Chapter 8: All Things Tied

This may be my favorite topic to discuss. In fact, I am sure I could write an entire book on oral ties alone. Let's start with me explaining just what a "tie" is. Everyone has a frenulum which is the stringy tissue under our tongue. This is a fiber that connects from the tip of our head all the way to our toes. What it means to be tongue tied or lip tied, is if the frenulum is connected in the wrong location causing restriction of the mobility of the tongue and lips. To better explain, everyone has the ligament that goes through the midline of the body and attaches our lip to the gumline, and our tongue to the floor of the mouth. If that ligament is too tight or tethered, or attaches in the wrong place of the mouth, this is referred to having an oral tie, aka tethered oral tissue.

If you haven't figured out by now, when it comes to helping new parents and babies, I am not afraid to rock the controversy boat. I believe strongly in continued research, continued learning, and, above all, fighting for what is right! Long before I was deemed the Booby Fairy, I was the tie queen. Okay, I was obviously more than just that, but for years I found myself fighting against my own training, my own gut instinct, just so I could comply with what the doctors above me were saying. However, something just didn't seem right. Doctors were claiming that tongue and lip ties were a "fad," or just a "money making scheme". However in my opinion, oral ties seemed to be more of an epidemic. I was seeing a lot of oral tethering in my practice and began to doubt myself.

How was it that almost every baby I was seeing had some form of poor oral structure? Then it dawned on me… I only see people with breastfeeding problems! Of course I was going to have a higher percentage in the private practice setting. When I was working in the hospital or even the pediatric office, I was seeing every baby, regardless of whether they were having feeding issues. Not every baby born is going to have a lip tie or tongue tie.

Yet as the years went on, and my private practice grew, the number of tied babies coming through my doors was doubling. Was I over diagnosing? Or could it truly be that there had been a significant increase in ankyloglossia (that is the fancy medical term for tongue tie)? I began questioning my skills, and then decided to do what I always do…when in doubt, check it out!

I poured myself into research. I got ahold of every book I could find, every webinar, workshop, and skills labs. If the breastfeeding world was about to change, I wanted to be part of it. I understood the controversy surrounding ties, especially in Orange County, Ca where we lived. We, as is providers in the mother baby world, all knew this was a growing problem.

The difficulty came in how to treat this, and at what age. This was not something that is taught in medical school to pediatricians or ENT doctors. While tongue ties are not new, only recently have we've realized how many problems are linked to them.

Doctors are given maybe five hours (and that is being generous) of breastfeeding training in school, and are only taught to look for anterior tongue ties that are extremely obvious. An anterior tie is when there is an extra growth of skin that connects the tip of the tongue to the gum line. We all knew that would create difficulty in speech and eating. Most would clip that with scissors, and symptoms would get somewhat better, though these kids would still have reflux, excessive crying, stomach pain which doctors will classify as "colic" which is just a term to describe unexplained crying, and gas. It was a start.

Dentists were actually the first to figure this out. They began noticing that children coming into their clinics with gaps in their teeth had also had a history of acid reflux and excessive crying as infants and had had difficulty breastfeeding. These kids were picky eaters and terrible sleepers with dark circles under their eyes. Most slept with their mouths open, and snored, resulting in bad breath.

The dentists also began noticing that kids with high arched palates also developed speech issues, sinus congestion, clogged teared ducts, and showed an increase in cavities under the front teeth due to lip ties. These kids also frequently had digestive issues, sleep apnea, and an increased need for orthodontic work, specifically palate expanders. Gaps in the teeth and crowding in the mouth seemed somewhat "common" in the dental world, but they were most certainly not normal. Dentists caught on and began opening up this new world of research. Why was this becoming a growing problem, and could it be prevented? This helped lead to the realization that oral ties were a big problem with many effects on children. The link of children who needed tubes in their ears from frequent ear infections, enlarged adenoids, again all had lip and tongue ties. Coincidence…or connection?

Unfortunately, most kids do not see a dentist until they are well into developing teeth. It would have never dawned on me before to take my brand new baby to a dentist for breastfeeding issues.

While dentists are trained in preventative care, pediatricians and other medical physicians are trained to wait for significant symptoms to appear before treating a disease. Preventative care for tongue ties/breastfeeding issues, which were unpredictable, was deemed risky or unnecessary. Why fix it if it isn't broken? Yet it is.

Ten to fifteen years ago, the methods used to treat oral restrictions were not great. The only options were scissors, which would only fix part of the problem, and it was way too risky to use them to treat lip ties or submucosal tongue ties. Frenotomy, which is a procedure that cuts into the muscle, required sedation and stitches. The diode laser was a better option. It was hot and required significant skill, and, again, wasn't able to fix the entire problem, but it was huge progress. Some turned to a cauldery scalpel, which basically just fried the tissue, and has no business in a baby's mouth. There were risks and the outcomes made pediatricians nervous, understandably so.

Frenectomy, which is the removal of the frenulum (the stringy part under the tongue) with a laser rather than a scalpel started to become popular since it was able to fix the ties without the need of anesthesia. This was incredible!

A bunch of dentists and doctors jumped on the frenectomy bandwagon, all seeking a way to revolutionize treatment for babies and kids. There is always a learning curve to treat medical conditions, and it seemed as if this newfound trend may have been doing more harm than good initially. Was it worth it?

I didn't just have a professional interest I this; I had a personal one as well. My youngest daughter was not thriving, despite the fact that I was doing everything I was being told to do by her pediatrician. I knew what I was seeing in my practice was different, and my mom gut was screaming at me to investigate. I had been trusting the doctor, all the while watching my kid suffer.

Alaina's story is complex but very common. I see the same scenario play out in my office with new mothers and their babies every day. When you see the same story repeat itself over and over again, you have to stop and pay attention.

When Alaina was born, as I mentioned in earlier chapters, she was a completely different baby then her sister. Alyssa was an easy baby, but Alaina cried and cried and cried. She had horrific acid reflux, to the point where she would spit up at least thirty times a day. (Yes, I absolutely counted one day.) Her doctor put her on Zantac (which we now know is dangerous for babies and has been linked to cancer), then Prevacid, and finally Prilosec. She never slept. She was "colicky" and gassy and continuously losing weight, and was just miserable all the time. I was made to feel as if all of her misery was my fault. The gaslighting that was done by so many doctors, specifically her pediatrician, was horrendous. Instead of investigating further, the doctor made me feel like I was the problem, that my milk was the cause of her digestive issues. How horrible for a new mom! I see this with practically every mom that walks through my office.

I had constant clogged ducts, mastitis, yeast infections, damaged nipples, vasospasms, and low supply. Alaina struggled to gain weight and was always in the fifth percentile for weight and the fifteenth percentile for height. Her doctor reassured me that was okay since she was consistent. She was not able to eat solids till she was over eight months old, and even then she was extremely picky. She didn't sleep through the night till she was almost four years old. She snored, was a mouth breather, and always had dark circles under her eyes. Sound familiar? Her doctor convinced me this was sinus related and that she needed nasal steroids.

154

At five years old she began experiencing ocular migraines. This poor kid was put under anesthesia four times before the age of six for MRI, MRA (when they are little, anesthesia is required), enlarged adenoids, and tubes in the ears. Again...I was trusting her pediatrician despite my mom-gut radar going off.

She had speech issues, ADHD, visual processing disorder, and had her first round of braces at age eight. She had three rounds of braces and palate expanders for a length of six years. Her orthodontist is the one who asked us to seek out help in assessing her ties.

She was fourteen the first time anyone seriously discussed her ties with me. The pediatrician had mentioned a lip tie when she was little, but told me not to worry, that she would most likely fall one day and split it open. Ummm...okay. Instead of fixing the problem correctly, we will just cross our fingers, hope and wait for a mouth injury to solve everything. Good gravy...cue my eye roll. The amount of times I hear doctors tell mothers that exact phrase is astounding. That is terrible medical advice!

I originally consulted with a pediatric dentist when she was in eighth grade, right around the year I began learning about oral ties. He treated her lip, but her posterior tongue tie also had a submucosal aspect, making it difficult for the diode laser to treat it correctly. Fixing her lip helped somewhat with the orthodontic aspect, but I still wasn't seeing her symptoms get much better. Not to mention that no aftercare was taught and it simply re-attached. I was beginning to understand why pediatricians were hesitant. We all knew this was a problem, but it was a problem that needed specific skills to treat and proper aftercare to prevent reattachment, which was not shown to us.

My daughter was so small that she was still in a car seat in 8th grade. Talk about social suicide in middle school! She had stopped growing and had fallen off the growth chart. This concerned everyone. Her pediatrician recommended growth hormones, and that is when I finally spoke up. The pediatrician (with good intent) had done enough to my kid. The lactation consultant in me took over, and I began to seek out other options.

Fast forward two years and my sweet girl was now sixteen years old. I just happened to be attending a lecture being given by a local pediatrician and children's dentist with thirty years' experience in oral ties. She was on the frontline of revolutionary new treatments, including the use of CO_2 lasers to treat ties. The only options I had learned about were frenotomy (this is the surgical incision into the tongue muscle to remove frenum and suture close), which I was not comfortable with, and frenectomy with a diode laser, which had originally only helped partially. So when the possibility of a new type of treatment arose, I was very intrigued. I attended the presentation and was blown away. Was it possible that a three-second procedure, with topical anesthetic, could really help my daughter and revolutionize her health? It was worth a shot so we made an appointment.

We both were slightly nervous but excited to see if this would help. She was in the laser room no more than ten minutes and was already feeling better when she came out. Was this too good to be true?

She was numb and hungry, and we headed home to begin fourteen days of stretches every four hours to help her heal. Naturally, she was sore, but it was more like muscle fatigue. She didn't love the stretches but knew they were important. At one point she looked at me and said, "Mom, I get that as my mother you have to do hard things to make me feel better, but I may say a four-letter word when you stretch my tongue!" I couldn't help but laugh. She was 100% right, though. Sometimes as parents we have to do hard things to better the health and quality of life for our kids. It sucks, and I didn't love knowing that this was hurting her, but I knew that it was the right call.

That night she slept. She slept through the night! It only took sixteen years. She was a whole new kid. What was even more amazing was that the kid who had not grown in two years grew over an inch in three weeks. I couldn't believe it. How was releasing a thick piece of skin so revolutionary for her growth and well-being? It was simple. The tongue is the one muscle in the body that continues to grow, and it can/will grow sideways. If there is a tongue tie of any sort, it can block the airway, making it impossible to get into REM sleep. If you don't get into a deep sleep, you can't grow. Not to mention that because of the tight midline tethering, it was more difficult for her to absorb her nutrients.

You have probably seen a snag in a sweater happen. If the thread is pulled, the fabric bunches together until you cut the thread and flatten out the cloth. This is exactly what it is like when the frenulum is released.

With Alaina's body able to rest and heal, she could finally give her body what she needed to grow and thrive. She was doing better in school, was happier and less moody, and was finally able to kiss her boyfriend. (That part we didn't share with Daddy, however.) I was blown away and had to learn more, so back to school I went. The more I learned, the more I knew my passion for healing was shifting.

I had developed severe migraines and TMJ disorder, and at the time of Alaina's release was suffering from a ten-day-long migraine that not even the ER could break. I had learned that adults with ties are more prone to sleep apnea and TMJ disorder. I was desperate, so I scheduled my own procedure. I was nervous, but I knew I had to practice what I preached. So there I sat at the young age of forty, about to get my submucosal tongue tie released. As it turned out, I actually had four ties and had grown extra bone in my mouth to compensate for what my tongue had been unable to do for years. I was flabbergasted.

I distinctly remember looking up at the ceiling, and within three seconds I heard a loud pop. My migraine was gone! I had instant relief in my jaw and lower back, and I was finally able to hear out of my right ear. I couldn't believe it. It felt like my head was floating, and all I could think was that if I felt this good immediately after, the babies must feel an incredible relief.

I was definitely sore, and needed my fair share of *Advil*, but I was in awe of how quickly I felt better. My jaw shifted, and even my husband noticed a difference (wink, wink). It was great to understand what the babies were feeling as well. I could now relate. My relief lasted a good 2-3 years, and then I noticed that some of my symptoms began to re-appear. Nervous and somewhat defeated, I went back to the drawing board of research. What I discovered was that the older the patient, the more muscle memory our body has created, and therefore needs to "pre-treat" with mayo-facial therapy. This isn't the case with every tie or older patient, but what I learned is that it is worth investigating on whether or not the type of tie you have requires before and after therapy depending on the degree and age of the patient.

With an anterior tongue tie, the tissue cannot stretch and therefore the tongue must be released prior. However, with posterior and submucosal ties sometimes suck therapy is needed to strengthen the underlying muscle to get the tongue as functional as possible so that the release will be effective.

When I was first trained in oral tethering, I was under the impression that all ties need to be cut regardless of age and type. Over time, especially when I opened up The Tongue Tie

Tribe with Dr. Rosanne Berger, DDS, IBCLC, Dr. Michelle Weaver, DC and Katie Byrum, SLP was that this is not always the case. I began to see the small percentage of babies that would have a frenectomy and not do well after. These cases required therapy from an OT (occupational therapist) or SLP (speech language pathologist). I always vowed that when it came to medicine I would always keep seeking and learning. What these ladies taught me, which I never saw before, was that with posterior tongues, getting the muscle functional was crucial, along with understanding any residual midline function. I asked Katie to explain her take on pre-therapy and ties for infants:

There is still much to learn about the development and make up of frenums as they move from typical to restrictive (tied). Whether ties are from a lack of cell death or overgrowth of tissue, they present early in development prompting dysfunctional sucking as soon as 15 weeks gestation. Loosely looking at an average 40 weeks of growth in utero, that is potentially 25 full weeks of aberrant motor patterns associated with this anatomical difference! And we haven't even covered the implications of birth trauma yet.

This is the starting point for every new baby I work with. Yes, there is the presenting anatomy but then I am immediately asking, Who is this baby? How was he or she conceived? grown? birthed? etc. While a tie cannot be stretched or "resolved," its initial visual appearance may be deceptive as there can be a collapse of tissue and space within the body based on the above. A brief look at the anterior fascial line and you quickly see how far the implications of that can travel within the body.

My job is to find baby's end range of expression (full range of motion), provide input for neuromuscular programming (touch the body for optimal movement and strength), and support releases when anatomy is no longer serving. As a Speech-Language Pathologist, we are trained to assess function first and foremost. It is incredible how major oral dysfunction can be associated with a very small anatomical tie. Conversely, a large, thick tie could go asymptomatic. My belief is there is untapped potential within the body that can be expressed with dynamic movements, energy changes, and manual manipulation before we know the core implication of a tie. And thus, we are ethically obligated to seek that babe's greatest potential before we alter his or her anatomy.

I would be remiss if I didn't address the different disciplines one may encounter on this journey. The role of rehabilitation therapists and subsequent intervention can be confusing to consumers and professionals alike. While Speech-Language Pathologists (SLP) often claim dominance over the crucial oral and pharyngeal (throat) structures needed for sucking and swallowing, some of the best infant feeding professionals I know are Physical Therapists (PT) who have taken a special interest in oral and respiratory function. The important thing is working with a provider who is well trained and treats a full body suck. Everything matters from the toes to eyebrows. If you are working with a therapist to prepare for a release and your SLP is not addressing the sacrum, your Occupational Therapist is not addressing extensor and flexion patterns, your PT is not working on lingual strength, look elsewhere.

- Katherine Byrum, SLP, CCC

I interviewed several different doctors about their explanation of the different types of ties and here is the best explanation I could make:

TONGUE TIES

Everyone has a tongue tie. The question we should be asking is if the tongue tie is restricting the function of the tongue muscle. The tie itself is a small band of tissue that connects the tongue to the floor of the mouth. It is made of collagenous fiber that does not stretch. The tissues and

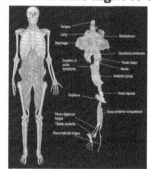

The Tongue Connects via Fascia Line Right to Toes

Tongue Posture Guides Core Stability Through Hips

muscles around the tie may stretch to accommodate the ties, but the actual tie does not stretch.

It should be located in the middle of the tongue and connect to the middle of the mouth floor. The tongue is attached to eight different muscles under the floor of the mouth. If the attachment is too far forward or too tight, then the tongue cannot function properly.

People often refer to this abnormality as being "tongue tied." Tongue ties can cause problems with breastfeeding because the tongue is restricted in its natural wave-like movement of sucking and feeding. They can cause nipple pain, latch problems, and poor weight gain. Many babies will bite instead of suck, or appear "chompy" as the child is using the lower jaw to lift the tongue since the muscle itself is incapable of moving on its own. They might make clicking sounds while feeding or swallow air and have gas or colic issues. They may also gag easily and have a shallow latch and pinch mom's nipple, causing what we call "lipstick nipples." If the tongue can not reach the roof of the mouth, the palate can not form correctly resulting in arched palates, shelf palates, which also impacts the development of the sinus which is often why some newborns who have ties have congestion in their nose and more frequent clogged tear ducts.

Different problems may also occur later in life, such as swallowing/gagging/eating problems, speech problems, breathing issues, and dental complications. There are even studies being done to see if ties could be related to the increase of ADHD in children due to the lack of proper sleep and oxygenation while the cortex of the brain is developing. Research shows that a tongue tie procedure is a safe and effective treatment and helps to improve breastfeeding.

The tongue is a very unique muscle. It is the only muscle in the body that is connected only on one side. Tongue ties cause problems with tongue function. Babies and children can often stick the tongue out and down. However, that is only one motion that is needed to breast and bottle feed efficiently, break down and swallow food, and speak clearly.

The posterior portion of the tongue needs to raise and lower in the back of the mouth and the sides of the tongue need to raise up to hold milk or food in the back portion of the mouth. The tip of the tongue also needs to come up just behind the teeth prior to swallowing.

Babies that are tongue tied often have a humped tongue in the back and a short front attachment to the gum line. This makes it hard to make the necessary wavelike motion and to create the vacuum suction to properly withdraw milk from the breast or bottle and to be able to swallow correctly.

When the tongue is humped in the back and the baby is lying down, they will often open their mouth to breathe better because of the airway obstruction from the tongue. Babies are obligate nose breathers so any breathing with an open mouth is NOT normal. Often parents will complain about chronic nasal congestion but there is no mucus in the nose. This

chronic congestion and difficulty breathing is actually the
noise of the tongue resting against
and obstructing the airway. These
babies will often be restless sleepers.
They are noisy breathers and active
sleepers. Some babies will even
learn to hyperextend their neck to
further open the airway and make

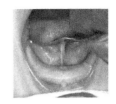

Tongue Tie prior to
release

breathing more comfortable. When babies do not sleep well,
they will be cranky and colicky during the day and not feed
well.

Older children will have behavior or attention problems.
Tied babies often later develop enlarged tonsils and adenoids
because of the forward position of the tongue and stunted
development of the mid-face, and have an increased chance
of ear infections, due to the inability for the eustachian tubes
being able to drain resulting in
surgical tubes being placed.

When the tongue forms on the
floor of the mouth, there is no
stopping mechanism for the palate,
so it continues to grow up and
become high and arched. Just
above the palate are the sinus
cavities. This arching of the
palate alters the development of

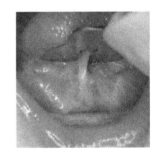

Submucosal tongue tie

White facia overlying frenulum

the sinuses and causes abnormal pooling areas to form, which can cause an issue with chronic runny noses and, later on, recurrent and chronic sinusitis.

Oral ties, specifically submucosal posterior tongue ties, can also result in torticollus (a condition in which the head becomes persistently turned to one side, often associated with pain and muscle spasms). This can also lead to plagiocephaly, or flat spots on the head, that in severe cases can result in the need of an infant helmet to help form the fontanels into the proper place. Cranial sacral therapy and chiropractic care can help with these conditions, but if a tie is present the body work will not hold.

There are different thought process in diagnosis of ties in regards to "levels" or "grades" 1-4 in severity. In my opinion, you either are tied or you are not. It has everything to do with the function. There are however different types of tongue ties. Anterior ties we have already discussed, which are what most doctors are trained to look for as these are visible. Posterior tongue ties are when the frenum   grows into the muscle impeding the function. These types of ties you have to feel, which is why a suck assessment is always necessary. White coating on the tongue or a shaking jaw is often the first sign as well as sucking blisters present on the lips. Sometimes, not often, a posterior tongue tie with the help of suck training can become functional enough to the point of not needing any intervention as a baby. I always express to the family however, that even with the improvement of the suck, there is the possibility of other ailments developing later in life, and to take that into consideration when deciding wether or not to treat.

Submucosal is when a white piece of fascia has grown over the posterior frenum. These are the most troublesome and often get missed. If your doctor is claiming that there is no tie despite your symptoms, and has not done a suck assessment, then seek another opinion. You can only diagnose these ties with feel. Submucosal ties are often the cause of babies loosing weight as the baby is burning more calories by trying to suck then they are gaining. Infant weight loss is rarely the fault of the mother's milk. You were designed to feed your baby. Your body will respond. Do not accept blame by a healthcare provider for your baby not gaining weight because of the claim that your milk is not enough. This is often not true. Seek a second opinion, especially if the baby has enough pees and poops.

TONGUE TIE TREATMENT

The procedure to snip or cut a tongue tie is called a frenotomy. The laser procedure to remove a tongue tie is called a frenectomy. At The Tongue Tie Tribe, we perform a frenectomy procedure using a CO_2 laser, after a consult to determine if the tongue is ready. Anterior ties have to be treated sooner than later as the tongue will not be able to function at all due to the tight band of tissue. These we try

167

and treat as soon as possible. Other forms of oral tethering however, we encourage some exercises to ready the mouth first.

Depending on the age of the baby, the child is first assessed by our IBCLC (myself) Chiropractor, or SLP to determine what kind of tie is present and if suck training is needed. If the baby is older than 10 weeks we need to determine if the suck reflex has integrated.

Between the age of 10-13weeks the suck reflex that has been present since 28weeks gestation, integrates or becomes habit vs reflex. This can make things more difficult if the baby has never had the ability to suck, or learned to suck because of a fast flow of milk from either mom or the bottle. We call this "riding the letdown". If the baby doesn't have to suck in order to feed, meaning they simply open their mouth because the flow is so fast, this can result in an underdeveloped suck pattern. This can also happen when parents are not pace feeding with the bottle and simply forcing the milk down the baby's mouth. Proper positioning is crucial for both ways of feeding. Ties are also a main reason why so many babies can not take a bottle. There is no prior instinct or knowledge of how to suck.

Many pediatricians will tell you that the tie isn't an issue because the baby is gaining weight. Of course the baby is gaining weight if the mother has an over-active letdown. The kid doesn't have to work at all. The problem will always shift around 3-4 months when all of a sudden the hormones shift and cause mom's supply to dip. If the baby has never learned to suck, this is when they begin to fall off the growth chart and end up in the hands of a feeding therapist to re-train the brain. This results in so much unnecessary frustration, time, and finances. This is why we encourage pre-therapy for all posterior tongue ties.

If the tongue is too weak, performing the frenectomy can result in a "floppy tongue" making feeding more difficult and painful. We advise at least one week of suck training for all posterior ties, sometimes more. In some cases seeing a feeding therapist may be wise. Suck training consists of resting your pointer finger in the palate of the baby's mouth to illicit the suck pattern. You may find that you have to stimulate the suck by tickling the palate. Once you feel the suck, with your other hand, pull the jaw down to force the tongue to lift and cup around the finger. The goal is to have the baby be able to sustain a seal for about 60% of the time, consistently for about 5 minutes. I recommend doing this about 4x a day for a week. When the tongue is "functional" enough or as well as it can be, the release will be far more successful. For a video guide on how to perform suck training, please visit our instagram page @tonguetietribe.

Using a CO2 laser is a safer, less painful, and a more complete way of releasing than clipping with scissors or heating and destroying the tissue with a diode laser. The CO_2 laser frenectomy is done in a laser-safe procedure room within our office. A study was recently published on how the use of lavender essential oil can reduce infant pain by 50%. (https://pubmed.ncbi.nlm.nih.gov/30915309/) That is an easy thing to do to relieve pain. You can always diffuse this in the baby's room, we have it constantly diffusing in our procedure room. Next one of our providers, usually myself, performs cranial sacral therapy as a way to help guide our dentist in the release, and ease some pain by increasing the flow of cerebral spinal fluid. The dentist often uses

a topical numbing agent prior to the procedure of lidocaine so the infant doesn't feel any pain. The baby will be swaddled in a papoose and goggles are placed to help

The procedure itself takes about three seconds and your baby can go straight to the breast or bottle afterward in our lactation room. Many mothers feel less nipple pain and a better latch almost immediately. Baby is often able to obtain a deeper latch and easily transfer more milk, in less time. What I have always found fascinating is during our procedures either myself or our amazing chiropractor Dr. Michelle Weaver will often do cranial sacral therapy to help guide Dr. Berger in knowing when the tension from the back of the cranium relaxes. It serves as a wonderful guide and limits the need for more intense therapy. As Dr. Weaver would say, it melts like butter!

LIP TIES

Just like a tongue tie, everyone has a lip tie. The question we should be asking is if the lip tie is restricting the function of the lip muscle. The tie itself is a small band of tissue (a frenulum) that connects the lip to the upper gum-line. It is made of collagenous fiber that does not stretch. The tissues and muscles around the tie may stretch to accommodate the ties, but the actual tie does not stretch. It should be located in the middle of the upper gum-line and connect to the lip close to the bony part of the gumline.

When the lip is flipped up to the nose using your index finger and thumb to hold on either side of the tie, the tie itself and the gumline attachments should stay pink and not turn white, which is called blanching. This should not be painful. If the attachment is short and tight or inserted near the middle or edge of the lip border, then the lip cannot function properly. In breastfeeding or bottle feeding, lips are solely meant to rest and create a soft seal to prevent air from entering. Babies should not have an upper lip muscle, which

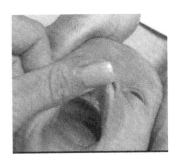

Grade 4 lip tie

171

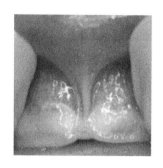

Grade 3 lip tie with cord blanching at gemlike

can form if the baby has been trying to use the lip to compensate for lack of tongue function, and sucking blisters or callouses that form are not normal, although common, and are often a tell tale sign of a lip tie. It is important to also know since the lip tie can be the most obvious to see, that 95% of the time if there is a lip tie there is also some form of a tongue tie. Suck assessments are a crucial piece to understanding the function of the mouth.

We often see babies grabbing onto the breast or bottle with the lip muscle and trying to move the lip in a wave-like rhythmic motion instead of using the tongue muscle. Normally, a thin lip muscle will develop with use of a spoon for eating solids and is used for some letters in speech like "P" and "B." A tight lip tie will cause the upper lip to pull up in the center and look more like a triangle. The abnormal triangular upper lip shape causes the mouth to rest open and makes it difficult to use the lip to form letters or eat solids. The younger this attachment is released, the more normal the lip forms and develops over time. It is always easier to look for a lip tie, so trained professionals tend to start there.

Lip ties can cause problems with breastfeeding because, when the lip is restricted, it can prevent the mouth from opening fully, which does not allow the tongue to feed correctly. Lip ties can cause nipple pain for mom, lip

172

blistering for baby, and persistent shallow latch problems. If the lips are not correctly sealed on the breast or bottle, baby will swallow a lot of air. Doing so causes excessive gas or colic issues. Different problems may also occur later in life, such as eating problems, speech problems, and dental issues. Lip ties cause sensory issues with eating. When the lip is pulled down and attached to the gumline, textured foods or even just the act of using the lip to remove food from a spoon is irritating and will cause a food aversion. If the lip tie covers the teeth, then it can be painful or hard to brush the teeth. This can cause an increased risk and incidence of cavities, gum irritation, and gum recession. Research shows that a lip tie procedure is a safe and effective treatment that decreases air swallowing and reflux issues related to the ties.

LIP TIE TREATMENT

The procedure to cut a lip tie is called a labial frenotomy. When scissors or a scalpel are used to cut a lip tie, it always bleeds because there is a thin layer of tissue over the tie. It is also difficult to remove all of the tie with scissors, and it often reattaches and forms a thicker, stronger tie. A revision of a scarred lip tie is much more challenging and painful, and frequently has more bleeding. Sometimes you will hear misinformed people say, "Just wait for it to tear on its own. Babies always fall and will eventually bust it open" This will never fix a lip tie, and again is horrible medical advice. Why are we waiting for a trauma to fix a problem? When a lip tie tears as a result of an accident or injury, the overlying tissue covering the thick collagenous fibers tear and most of the actual lip tie is still present. This goes against putting the well being and safety of the patient first. Healthcare providers take an oath to at first do no harm no one should ever recommend injuring yourself to fix the problem as appropriate medical advice or treatment. When the tissue rips under pressure, it is very painful and bloody, often requiring an emergency room visit. It is much safer to release the tie in a controlled environment with a laser that will also minimize bleeding.

The laser procedure to remove a lip tie is called a labial frenectomy, and it is also performed with the use of a CO_2 laser, which helps control pain and aid in healing. The procedure itself takes a few seconds, and your baby can go straight to the breast or bottle afterward. Remember, your baby does not need their lip to feed, but they will be a bit confused with a numb lip while latching. Many mothers feel less nipple pain and a better latch almost immediately. After the procedure, some infants

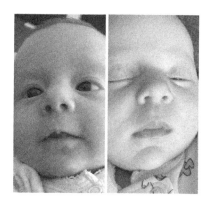

Left is prior to lip tie procedure
Rt picture is 20 min after lip frenectomy

may feel pain for one to three days, which can be managed.

174

Although it is a minor procedure, as with any surgical intervention, it does have some risks, including but not limited to bleeding, pain, allergic reactions, temporary numbness, injury to the mouth, scarring, or reattachment. Most of which can be relieved with some extra snuggles and skin to skin from mom and if needed, based on age the use of tylenol/Genexa or medical grade clove oil, diluted with fractioned coconut oil to naturally numb the area. Clove is a hot oil so it should be 3 drops to a ratio of 2ml. You shouldn't put just any type of essential oils in a mouth, in fact most do not belong in or near an infant. It must be a legit, regulated, medical grade formula such as DoTerra or Young living, to make it safe for the baby.

BUCCAL/CHEEK TIE

A buccal tie is a small band of tissue, a frenulum, that connects the cheek to the upper or lower gumline. It is made of collagenous fiber that does not stretch. The tissues and muscles around the tie may stretch to accommodate the ties, but the actual tie does not stretch. The more that the cheek muscle is used, the stronger and bigger the tie will become. If the tie is up high to the cheek bone but some tension is present, then in some instances, massaging the masseters (the medical name for the cheek muscle) can help loosen the tension. To do this take your pointer finger and massage inside the baby's cheek from the top all the way down to the bottom of the cheek making a "C" with your finger. Doing this motion several times a day will help tremendously in loosening and prepping the muscle for proper release.

The cheek muscles on either side of the nose will get stronger and larger as well. This puts pressure up against the eyes and makes it more challenging to smile. It also does not feel good when your face is tight and muscular. We want soft and squishy, kissable cheeks. It should not hurt to pull your cheek out and you should not feel anything along your gumline when you rub the upper and lower gums. Many providers who have not been

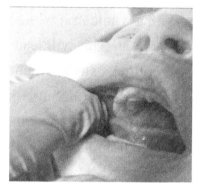

Cheek tie with lip blisters

educated about cheek ties do not know how to assess for a buccal tie or make this diagnosis. This is why it is important to see a provider trained to diagnosis and release these ties.

In breastfeeding or bottle feeding, cheeks are solely meant to rest and guide milk back to the posterior tongue, which lowers during a swallow. When cheeks are used to suck, instead of the tongue, more air is brought in and swallowed. This leads to gas, reflux symptoms, and colic issues. The suck of the cheeks can often be seen while nursing as a depression or dimpling from where the tie is attached. It can often be painful for mom and baby as well. Some babies

176

suck so hard with the cheeks that they collapse the nipple of the breast or bottle like a straw and cannot get milk, which is frustrating. This can make the nipple look lipstick shaped or flat when done breastfeeding. The harder babies suck with their cheeks, the less milk comes out, which is frustrating for mom and baby, and leads to weight loss from excess calorie burn. It is literally like sucking a milkshake through a straw with a whole in it while running on a treadmill. Talk about a work out! This will lead to a slowly decreasing milk supply over time, usually when the baby is three to five months of age, primarily because the breast works by milk removal and hormones. After the 3 month marker milk supply is based off of milk removal. If you have a baby who can not properly drain a breast because of poor suction, then the supply goes down and the frustration of the baby goes up.

Different problems may also occur later in life. Children will often use the side of their tongue with the cheek tie to pocket food, then chew and swallow the food. This is a very inefficient way to eat as it takes a long time to break down food this way in the mouth or in the stomach itself. This leads to digestive issues and constipation. It can also be painful to smile and laugh because of the tension in the tie. It becomes difficult and painful to brush and floss with the ties in the way. Children are also at increased risk of cavities between these teeth because the tie will hold milk or small pieces of food in the area. The buccal ties will also push the teeth out of alignment or prevent the secondary teeth from coming in properly.

Buccal ties cannot be safely released with scissors or scalpel or with a diode laser, as it is too hot and painful and causes scarring in the area. A CO_2 laser, which we use at our office, is necessary for this procedure. The procedure itself takes one to two seconds and your baby can go straight to the breast afterwards. Many mothers feel less nipple pain with a softer latch and a strong tongue suck almost immediately.

I cannot stress enough the importance of aftercare after the release of a tie. This is something the practitioner who is releasing the ties should teach you. The aftercare—the stretches and bodywork that follow—are absolutely the key to preventing a reattachment. I see reattachment much more frequently in those that were not taught how to do appropriate aftercare, or the parents were to nervous to stretch deeply. Think of it like a paper cut. (We have all had those at one time or another and if you haven't, dude share your secret because I get them all the time!) If you apply pressure to the paper cut it doesn't feel great but it doesn't really hurt either. If you gently touch a paper cut it stings. This is a great analogy.

The stretches are the most important part, and the firmer you are the less painful it is. I learned that the hard way when I had my own frenectomy. I remember sitting in traffic trying to do the stretch and realizing that the deeper and firmer I stretched, the less it stung. In those instances it can definitely

178

be mind over matter. Especially when it comes to stretching your own kids. I have no problem stretching my patients, but when it came to stretching my daughter, yikes! I did not like it. But as I said before, as a parent you will have to do many things that are not pleasant for the child, but are incredibly important for their wellbeing. Parenting is not for the weak!

How to do the stretches:
- For at least two weeks, the sites need to be stretched every four hours, including at night (you may be able to go longer at night after the first forty-eight hours
- Make sure you are using clean hands or gloves
- Apply diluted clove oil with fractioned coconut oil on your finger or under the tongue to numb the area so the stretch does not sting. You can make your own. It typically is 3 to 5 drop ratio of clove vs coconut oil. Under the tongue you will see a diamond-shaped wound. (If you would like to see pictures, or a video they are available on my website.) Going along the corners of the diamond, march firmly like you are making a pie crust, making sure to focus on the corners. It may bleed and that is okay. The mouth is vascular. Just like how we sometimes bleed when we floss, this will happen at times during the stretch. It will most likely look like more blood then there actually is because it will mix with the saliva
- Start at the gumline and swoop down and up with your index finger, pushing against the wound and rolling up.

You can also use both index fingers and lift under the tongue to elevate. I recommend alternating fingers each stretch to provide even pressure. For example, because we recommend stretching every four hours, on the even stretches use your right index finger and on the odd stretches use your left index finger.

• For the lip: Place your index finger under the lip and swipe back and forth like a windshield wiper, three times. Then lift the lip up all the way towards the nose and rub. After use both fingers to physically curl the lip up towards the nose.

• For the buccal/cheek: Apply firm pressure on the sites for three seconds and rub back and forth

• If you see yellow or white strings forming under the tongue or lip, swipe through and break those formations. We want the wound to heal slowly and correctly. As the scabs form, swoop through and lift.

• If a granuloma forms after the two-week marker, dry under the tongue with a piece of gauze, and use vitamin E oil on the area. Granuloma is basically a small ball of scar tissue. It can soften over time.

A palate stretch as demonstrated in this picture is specifically helpful with babies who have high arched palates that are present most likely from posterior tongue ties. This exercise helps to stretch the palate to a better formation as well as ease nasal congestion

Arched Palate Stretches

that occurred from the tension of the ties. To do this, take both index fingers and stretch the palate out towards the jaw with firm pressure for about 5-10 seconds. It actually feels really good and babies love it!

Another key factor to healing is bodywork. This can be done with the help of a trained chiropractor who is skilled in frenectomy treatment and infants, with a craniosacral therapist, or with an infant physical therapist. Baby chiropractic care is super gentle and probably the most effective in healing. It is not what you would imagine— definitely no cracking of necks like you see on adults. It literally looks like a form of infant massage, but it helps with the healing of the sites as the muscles figure out where to go and can also aid in decreasing reflux symptoms and can help the baby poop. To help further explain the impact chiropractic care can have on a baby's quality of life, specifically after a tongue tie release, I asked my favorite chiropractor, and beloved friend Dr. Michelle Weaver, to explain:

Babies can experience various physical complications during the birth process, which can cause babies to have spinal misalignments and develop muscle tension. The muscle tension and spinal misalignments can cause colic (extreme fussiness), torticollis (muscle asymmetry in the neck where baby

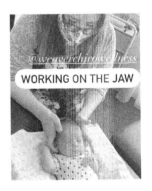

WORKING ON THE JAW

181

favors rotation to one side), and reflux, among others. Chiropractic care can provide optimal nerve connection between the brain and body; the brain connects to the spinal cord and the spinal cord connects to muscles, skin, and organs.

Because babies have less well developed muscular and skeletal systems, they respond well to the gentleness of infant chiropractic work, which is quite different than the approach that is seen with adults. Diversified chiropractic adjustments for adults are high-velocity, low-amplitude thrusts that sometimes can cause a cavitation or "pop" sound. The "pop" sound (like when one is cracking their knuckles) is actually CO_2 being released from the joint space. Chiropractic adjustments to babies are considered low velocity and low amplitude; this means the adjustments are gentle and there is never a cavitation sound or "pop." The amount of pressure that is applied is the same as the pressure you would apply to the skin of a tomato before the skin breaks.

Infant chiropractic adjustment

During the first chiropractic visit, we assess the baby's range of motion, deep tendon reflexes, and primitive reflexes, and conduct an orthopedic exam to assess baby's musculoskeletal health. Primitive reflexes are present at birth and

182

eventually disappear; examples of primitive reflexes are Moro's reflex (the startle reflex) and sucking reflex. Babies learn to suck in utero, but not all babies are able to suck properly and may have dysfunctional suck patterns due to tethered oral ties and/or jaw misalignment from the birthing process.

Tethered oral restrictions (tongue ties, cheek ties, and lip ties) are considered midline issues and therefore it is not uncommon for babies with tethered oral ties to have other midline issues, which include but are not limited to increased muscle tension in the neck and upper back, torticollis, reflux, and digestive issues. When the tethered oral tie restriction is removed during a frenectomy, tension can still exist, and chiropractic care can help to release the tension that was associated with the anatomical restrictions relating to the ties.

– Dr. Michelle Y. Weaver, DC
Weaver Chiropractic Wellness

Craniosacral therapy is another wonderful modality that focuses mainly on the stretching and massage of the fontanels and cranial nerves. It helps the baby release tension as the fontanels (the bony plates in the baby's head) begin to suture together. The beautiful thing about chiropractic

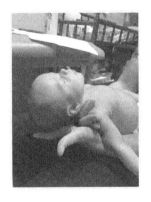

Guppy Hold

183

care or craniosacral therapy is that there are exercises that can

Torticollis stretch with suck training

be taught to the parents to practice at home. I do have several examples of this in a video form on my Instagram and website for your review. Pacifiers, although controversial, are crucial in the healing of frenectomy, in my opinion. However, the type of pacifier matters.

Personally, I prefer MAM newborn pacifiers. This specific pacifier allows the lips to flange and strengthen in the correct way. The point of the pacifier is to train the mouth and muscles to operate in a way that moves the milk from the nipple correctly. We look at pacifier use as a form of PT. Most babies need training, as they are not all fans of the pacifier. I want to reassure you that there is not going to be an issue of nipple confusion. Nipple confusion isn't really a thing. It is flow preference that can cause problems. Since baby needs to "chew to poo," it is important to offer the pacifier after feeding to aid in digestion. Not every baby needs this to

Torticollis stretch

184

poop, but babies who have been tongue tied and have an arched palate will benefit.

Rub the pacifier on the roof of the mouth to trigger the suck reflex. Angle the baby onto the tummy so that gravity helps the tongue to fall forward and the cheeks to work to keep the pacifier in. Playing a little tug-of-war will allow the baby to work to keep the pacifier in place.

The concern that some providers have with pacifier us is that, in the beginning, new parents may confuse feeding cues for suck need, and therefore a brand new baby will not feed as often as needed. When offered after a feed, it can be very beneficial. In regards to orthodontic concerns, it really has no effect. The formation of the palate and teeth often has more to do with the structure of the cheek and tongue ties than the use of pacifiers. This is why the Nuk or "orthodontic" pacifiers are not favored, as they compound the compression and malformation of the palate.

If the parent is concerned about the pacifier as a habit, it can always be taken away. Most children suck to soothe, and if the pacifier is not there, the thumb is usually an option. I had a thumb-sucking kiddo and a pacifier babe. The thumb sucker sucked her thumb well into elementary school. Her braces is what finally broke her of that habit. My pacifier kiddo (embarrassingly, she was two years old when I finally took the pacifier away, but, hey, I worked nights, and this momma needed sleep) was a lot easier to break. We tied her pacifier to a helium balloon and sent it to baby Jesus. Sometimes as parents you have to get creative.

Post frenectomy, some form of suck training is important. Some providers suggest myofascial work prior to a tie release. This truly depends on the age of the patient and the type of tie. If the baby has a posterior tongue tie suck training prior to the release is crucial. If it is an anterior tie, therapy before may not be helpful. If the child is old enough to understand myofascial exercises or the adult who has had years of muscle memory to work out, therapy prior is very helpful. This is why each case of a tongue tied patient is unique and needs to be evaluated with an individual plan of care.

After the release, the tongue is weak, and the baby is trying to relearn how to suck, which is where the art of suck training comes into play. If the parent is uncomfortable using a pacifier, a clean finger can be used. Prior to latching:

1. Hold your baby in your lap in a sitting position, supporting the head in the palm of your hand
2. With clean hands, or using a glove, insert your free index finger, palm side up, into your baby's mouth, resting comfortably in the soft curved

Suck Training with acupressure

186

palate on the top part of the mouth. Be careful not to insert your finger too far into the baby's mouth, as this can cause him to gag. Simply go as far as the first knuckle joint. The tip of your finger should be touching the palate, which feels "squishy" on the roof of the mouth. If you find that the palate is high and arched, that is a good indication that there is a posterior tongue tie.

3. Gently stroke the roof of your baby's mouth to encourage the infant to begin sucking. Once you feel your baby sucking on your finger, extend your finger straight.

4. Your baby should be wrapping the sides of his/her tongue around your finger. With your finger straight (applying gentle pressure onto the back of the tongue), pull down on the baby's lower lip.

The baby's tongue should be on the floor of his mouth with the sides of his tongue curled against your finger. After you have checked the position of the tongue, make sure that the lips are rolled out around the

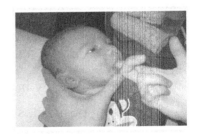

Suck Training with jaw extension

finger as well. If the baby's lips appear to be tucked in, do your best to flange them out. After a lip tie revision, they should flange out like a fish. If they are not able to because

187

a restriction is still there, then I would follow up with the doctor who performed the frenectomy.

5. Allow the baby to suck on your finger for one to two minutes while pulling down on the chin to help the tongue extend out further. Gently push down and forward with your finger while the baby is sucking.

6. Once you feel that the baby's tongue has relaxed into a down and forward position and has a good sucking rhythm, your baby should be ready to latch onto the breast. Be sure to have good pillow support. Bring the baby to your breast and lean back when latching.

Now let's talk about re-attachment. Obviously the goal is to do everything within our power to not have the frenum re-attach or become tight in the wrong area. There will be some frenulum band that forms, but the hope is that it forms in a position that allows the tongue and lips to be functional. Frenum has a purpose, we just have to make sure that purpose serves the mouth and body well. There are some things you can do to help prevent re-attachment from happening.

1. The most important thing you can do is stay on top of the aftercare. The after care stretches, and massage that follows for 3 months is crucial. It is so easy to slack off and think it isn't necessary. The last thing you want is to have to put the baby through another procedure because the aftercare stretches were not done correctly. I know it sucks, but as a parent we have to do hard things to make our

babies well. I guarantee it will not be the last time you have to do something with or to your child that is difficult but in their best interest.

2. Avoid the *snoo*!! We are not fans of the *snoo* and I know so many of you are dying a slow exhausted death inside hearing that. The thought process behind this expensive bassinet does work in the sense of keeping the baby sleeping longer or appearing to sleep longer. However that isn't what is best for the child. The *snoo* pins down the baby's mid back and arms to the sides of their body and increases tension from head to foot. Time and time again the cases if reattachment or overall body tension have all had one thing in common. The arms were pinned down and swaddled to their sides. This causes and continues to create tight fascia that releases with bodywork but returns after being placed back into the *snoo*.

3. Make sure that you continue with bodywork, and suck training. Practice makes perfect in this scenario and is well worth the time spent to provide a better quality of life for your little ones.

As a new parent it can be incredibly frustrating to hear conflicting advice from many different healthcare providers. You just want to do what is best for your little one. So who do you trust? When there is not a clear answer on a new and evolving medical treatment plan, my best advice, besides trusting your parental gut, is to research trusted sources, ask other parents who have been through this before, and talk to you partner. At the end of this book there are several studies sited as well as listed on our website www.tonguetietribe.com

When you BOTH are on the same page on the care and treatment of your baby, then you can move forward feeling confident in your decisions to better your baby's health. Your provider should be skilled in understanding the importance of pre and post therapy for any form of oral tethering. Ties are not cookie cutter, not all are the same, and every case should be taken individually with a care plan that works for everyone to achieve the best possible outcome life long.

Chapter 9: MTHFR

It would be careless of me not to talk about the notorious MTHFR gene mutation (what we call the mother "effing" gene) after discussing oral tethering. There is definitely much debate and a crazy ton of research about this gene mutation. What we know is that this is more common than previously thought and a big reason why we have seen an increase in oral ties. Doctors would be remiss if they do not take the time to learn more about how this is affecting our population and our children, specifically in the areas of breastfeeding, growth, and development. Medicine is always evolving, so I cannot fault doctors for not knowing what certain conditions are if they have not been taught, but I can fault them for not continuing their education and exploring other possibilities. The fact is there has been an increase in the prevalence of this mutation, and we are starting to understand why.

MTHFR stands for methylenetetrahydrofolate reductase, and it is an enzyme that is responsible for multiple functions in the body. When you hear someone say they have MTHFR, they generally mean they have an SNP, "single nucleotide polymorphism." SNPs are what scientists call mutations that occur within DNA.

It has been said that as many as 40% of people have some form of the MTHFR mutation. Some people may have no symptoms at all, while others have more serious complications like increased risk for heart disease, hormone imbalances, miscarriages, psychiatric conditions, digestive issues, and tongue ties. Children may have an increased risk for ADHD, learning disabilities, autism, or autoimmune disorders. Not everyone who inherits the mutation will have a problem, but they could pass it onto their children.

MTHFR gene type C677t leads to a reduced ability to convert folic acid into an active form of L-methylfolate. This masks a vitamin B12 deficiency and makes the individual more prone to bipolar disorder, depression, anxiety, OCD, and other conditions. Being vitamin B-12 deficient can make you tired, pale, irritable, and depressed, and can cause heart palpitations, easy bruising, nerve sensitivity such as pins and needles or tingling, digestive disorders, lightheadedness, and dizzy spells.

Carriers of this gene need to have methylated folate, as they have a difficult time processing folate or folic acid in its organic form. Because people with his gene mutation cannot convert folic acid into folate, they have a higher folic acid supply in the system. During organogenesis (the formation of organs in the uterus), this may enhance tissue synthesis with tighter closure of midline structures such as ankyloglossia, otherwise known as tongue and lip tie. Of all the midline defects, tongue tie tends to be the most common. Luckily, this can be treated as soon as the week of birth creating a better quality of life. Yay for science!

The debate is whether this is a new discovery of a problem that has been around since the beginning of time, or is it in fact a brand new problem developed from the mutating gene? Regardless, it is an issue that needs paying attention to. I believe that as medicine and science progresses, so does the skill of IBCLCs and other health care providers who have diligently sought out the training for identifying these underlying conditions.

Some doctors are choosing not to stay up to date with new research and studies supporting this increase, instead perceiving this as a fad or a money-making trend. Sadly, in healthcare I see this a lot, and as new parents you will encounter this constantly. There are many physicians that either feel pressure to give a diagnosis or feel that because they are "the doctor" with the medical degree, they cannot possibly be wrong. How dare we as parents or individuals challenge their knowledge base. It is okay to say you don't know. All we are asking is that the provider look into it instead of dismissing us immediately.

By dismissing this, doctors miss the chance to compensate for the folate absorbency issues in the mother, which could reduce the number of oral ties we see. If they are aware that the mutation is present, they can immediately look for and treat the ties that develop, understanding that there is an increased chance these babies will have them.

Being a carrier of MTHFR puts you at a higher risk for lifelong ailments and breastfeeding challenges, but there are treatment plans, including the use of nutrition and diet to help heal our bodies. If you feel like you are experiencing any of the symptoms of the MTHFR mutation, consult with your doctor about a simple blood test to find out. Sometimes just understanding the why makes all the difference in the world.

Chapter 10: When Formula Can Be Medicine

I remember waking up three days after giving birth and turning over to see my beautiful daughter glowing like an Oompa Loompa. I know I live in California, and suntans are in, but not when you are brand new! This kiddo had quite the color change. Sure enough, she had jaundice. Noticing your little one turning from plump and pink to yellow and mellow can be alarming! The good news is that jaundice is very common, easily diagnosed, and easily treated.

Jaundice is an overproduction of bilirubin, the chemical our body produces in order to break down red blood cells. Bilirubin is a yellowish pigment that is made during the normal process of breaking down red blood cells. In the uterus, the baby required more red blood cells to help prepare their body for the birth process. Although the liver is fully developed at birth, it isn't quite at its most efficient state. Sometimes there is a bit of a "traffic jam" at the liver as their little bodies try to pass the extra unneeded cells. Because our bodies are smart, they will push those cells to the skin surface to protect the organs from being stained, in hopes that UV rays from the sun will help break down the cells into smaller particles, thus producing the yellow tint. This is known as physiological jaundice.

Let me explain it this way. Imagine jaundice like a traffic jam. Let's say you are late for work, and if you are late one more time your boss is going to write you up. So you hop on the freeway just in time to notice the bumper to bumper traffic going on for miles. So you decide to take side streets to get to work on time. It isn't the ideal choice, but it will get the job done. If there is construction on the side streets, you may have to take the dirt road, which often is bumpy and dangerous and should be prevented. Jaundice is just like that. Bilirubin breaking down the red blood cells is the traffic jam (freeway) of the liver. Our body is smart, so it takes the "side streets" aka the skin to help protect the internal organs from being stained and damaged. In severe cases, the body will take the "dirt road" to the brain. If the brain becomes stained, brain damage can occur. The good news is that jaundice rarely progresses that far. It is so easily diagnosed, and easily treated. Physiological jaundice is not harmful if caught early and may last up to a week. Jaundice usually appears around day three of life and will peak on day five of life.

Direct Coombs–related jaundice is a bit different. At birth, your baby will have many blood tests, one of them being a Coombs test. The infant's blood is taken from the cord or a heel stick (which may happen often that first week) to check for a reaction between the mother's blood and the baby's blood, which can happen if mother and baby don't share the same Rh factor. Part of your routine prenatal care is to determine what blood group you belong to. A, B, AB, O along with deciphering if you are Rh negative or positive. This is important for the safety of the baby.

If the mother is Rh negative and the baby is Rh positive, the mother's blood will recognize the difference and may produce antibodies that can cross over to the baby's blood stream via the placenta, and destroy or weaken the infant's red blood cells. The Coombs test is used to detect this attack. If there is a positive Coombs test, the baby has a significantly higher chance of developing high jaundice levels. These cases of jaundice may call for a more specialized level of care, such as phototherapy, but are often noticed within the first twenty-four hours after birth.

Breastmilk jaundice appears the same way, but lasts much longer, and the baby can appear to be "yellow" for several weeks. In this scenario, the extra red blood cells are coming from mom and being passed through the breastmilk. Baby ingests them and the body then reacts. This is not harmful at all, and it is perfectly safe to continue to breastfeed. In fact, it is encouraged, as this will allow the baby's system to adapt. If the baby is still appearing yellow four weeks in, a repeat blood level is recommended to make sure that it is in fact breastmilk jaundice from the mother shedding blood cells versus an issue with the baby's liver.

If the baby is born jaundiced, that is concerning as that typically is an abnormality within the liver. This is extremely rare, however, and, if it were to happen, the doctors would be able to catch it instantly.

Close monitoring is very important with any form of jaundice as your baby can become extremely lethargic. In most cases, with an increase of fluids and food, the body will respond and pass the excess cells. Minor jaundice often is nothing to worry about as long as the baby is getting food. The only way to get rid of the extra bilirubin is to poop it out. Dead red cells is what makes our poop brown. The more you know… So again the babe must "chew to poo." The problem, however, is that baby often is too tired to eat, so it becomes a catch-22. Can't poop unless you eat, can't eat if you are sleepy. It can become very frustrating.

Some pediatricians recommend doing a "formula flush." This involves giving the baby 2 ounces of formula every two hours for twenty-four hours, until they have the energy to breastfeed. If there is less bilirubin needing to be expelled and fewer blood cells to break down, less energy is used. This is a perfect example of how, at times, formula can be considered medicine. This is especially true in the case of a direct Coombs case before mom's mature milk has surged in. The formula helps to push out that pesky bilirubin.

Here are a few breastfeeding-friendly tips to help treat and eliminate newborn jaundice:

1. First step is to speak to your child's pediatrician. They will most likely do a quick blood test to see just how high the bilirubin levels have become. If the levels are

mild then most likely just increasing the baby's food and exposing to indirect sunlight will do the trick.

2. Feed your baby every two hours during the day and every two and a half to three hours at night. This time starts from the start of the last feed. So if you fed at 8 a.m., start the next feed at 10 a.m. It will seem like all you are doing is breastfeeding, but it is VERY important that the baby receives enough fluids and food to flush out the bilirubin. A goal of ten to twelve feeds a day would be best.

3. Most likely the jaundice will make the baby very sleepy, so it may be tricky to wake them up. Undress the baby and place him in between your breasts, or at the breastaurant. This will help wake the baby up. If needed, wipe the baby down with a wet cloth or change their diaper. If you are unable to rouse the baby, contact the baby's pediatrician for further evaluation.

4. Monitor the baby's pees and poops. I know you feel like you are already monitoring a lot of things, but the baby's output is important. There is an app for that! By day six, the baby should have six wets and three to four poops in a twenty-four-hour period. You may notice that the urine has a rust color to it, what we call "brick dust." This is the excess red blood cells passing and should not be a cause for alarm unless it lasts for several days. The poop should be a yellow mustard seed color. If the baby is not peeing or pooping, you may need to supplement

with formula, as it may be an indication that your milk supply is delayed or has not surged in completely.

5. If you notice you are not producing enough milk to help treat the jaundice levels, consult with a lactation consultant near you who may set you up on a temporary triple feed program designed to help increase your milk supply, while also giving extra milk to the baby. A triple feed program is when a mother breastfeeds for fifteen minutes, then pumps for ten minutes, then supplements with expressed milk or formula. This is not a long-term solution, and it can be exhausting, so make sure your IBCLC gives you an end date for the triple feeds. Your pediatrician or lactation consultant may suggest using formula as a form of "medicine" if you do not have enough breast milk at the time. Obviously, breast milk works best, but the most important thing is to feed the baby so she can start pooping out the bili!

6. Keep the baby skin too skin, as this will help regulate the baby's natural rhythms, stabilize the infant's temperature, and release extra oxytocin to increase milk supply.

7. In severe cases, photo therapy may be recommended. Photo therapy is the use of ultraviolet lights to break down the cells. Some hospitals still require the baby to be admitted into the hospital for a UV incubator if the bili levels are higher than fifteen. Baby will have adorable little eye goggles and will be monitored

closely. Your little one is placed under the lights continually for twenty-four hours, only removed for feeds. In some less severe cases, depending on insurance and your provider, a bili-blanket can be used. The great news is that can now be done at home! It looks very similar to a sleeping bag. Baby is tucked in snugly, and the blanket emits ultraviolet rays that break down the bilirubin so it can be passed through her body more easily. This way the maternal/infant bonding is not interrupted and breastfeeding can be continued. Your doctor should have more information on that should it be needed.

Hypoglycemia or low blood sugar in the infant would be an additional reason for introducing formula within the first few days of life, as a form of medicine. This is more common in babies born from a diabetic mother and can happen 25–40% of the time, but it can happen to any baby, especially those having difficulty regulating their body temperature. This is one reason why skin-to-skin contact is so important within the first hour of birth. If that baby is cold, mom's body will heat up to keep that kiddo warm and not allow the blood sugar to drop. Typically, these baby's appear "jittery," which is a major red flag to nurses. If low blood sugar is suspected, a quick heel stick will determine the level. Anything below 40mg/dl is reason for concern.

Standard treatment for asymptomatic infants would be to initiate breastfeeding by one hour of age, followed by hourly feeds for at least four hours until the blood sugar stabilizes, then every two to three hours for the next twelve hours. If the mother does not have enough expressible colostrum or there is a separation between mom and babe, making it difficult to latch, then offering formula as "medicine" is needed in order to prevent the baby needing more aggressive treatments.

In some cases, glucose gel may be given in the buccal pads (cheeks) of the baby to prevent the need for IV glucose and NICU admission. A lactation consultant should come in to help guide you in bringing your milk in faster so that formula is not needed long term.

It is not recommended to give sugar water for the rapid absorption and increase in insulin. Your doctor, however, may use sugar water as a form of pain relief for babies three weeks and under for any procedure such as circumcision, frenectomy, or blood draws. Research has shown that sugar water is actually a better anesthetic then lidocaine and most pain relievers. Sugar is a powerful drug. No wonder kids of all ages love it so much.

The most important thing to remember is that the more you feed your baby during this time, the faster they will heal. Remember, you know your baby better than anyone, so trust your gut if you feel something isn't right. In the meantime, keep that baby close and enjoy every moment.

It may be weird to hear an IBCLC talk about formula, but in some instances it is necessary, and a mother should never ever be made to feel guilty about how she feeds her baby. Yes, we know that breast is best, but if for some reason you need to give a supplement of formula, it is okay. Please never feel ashamed of how you feed your little one. There are very valid reasons some women need to offer supplementation. It does not make you any less of a mom. Don't listen to that lie. You are a GREAT mother, and you are doing what is best for your baby.

Chapter 11: Induced Lactation

Becoming a mother is one of life's greatest joys. It is the hardest job you will ever have and by far the most rewarding. However, the adventure of getting to motherhood is sometimes a journey in and of itself. Infertility is on the rise, and getting pregnant for some just isn't written in the stars. IVF, IUI, months of trying, more months of disappointing negative pregnancy tests—it is a ridiculously difficult journey. Some women will eventually become mother's biologically, where others use surrogacy or adoption. Whichever route you take to become a new mommy, your baby will 100% be yours. What a gift!

We all know that breastfeeding is always encouraged and a very strong option for biological mothers who physically give birth to their children. However, what adoptive mothers or mothers who have used surrogates may not know is that they don't have to miss out on breastfeeding their babies as well.

Many women are able to successfully breastfeed their infants, even if they have never been pregnant before. How, you might ask. Well, we as mammals have been blessed with the anatomy, and all we have to do is stimulate and trick your body into producing. Even men can lactate!

There is a beautiful story of a father in Sir Lanka whose wife died giving birth to their twin babies. They were in a remote area, with no access to clean water. As he worked through his grief, he held those babies skin to skin and calmed them by chest feeding. His love for his children overpowered nature, and he actually started too lactate and was able to save his kids. Talk about a beautiful story of nature versus nurture. Some people have an issue with this, but our bodies are incredible. What a beautiful example of love and sacrifice.

(And, yes, I have made a man lactate before. I will save that story for my next book. Although, I can't tell you how many times I threatened to sprinkle Booby Fairy dust on my husband just so he could share the load. He was not a fan of that idea.)

Induced lactation, otherwise known as adoptive nursing, is the process of stimulating a woman's body to produce milk, even if she has never given birth or ever been pregnant. Yes, it is a lot easier to accomplish lactation when the pregnancy hormones are in place already, but that doesn't mean that you can't try and stimulate the production.

The success of induced lactation has a lot to do with your relationship with your new infant, and the age of the baby when you begin nursing. There is more to breastfeeding than feeding. Your bond with the baby has more of a hormonal effect then the amount of milk that is produced. Most women can make some amount of breast milk, and some will have an adequate full milk supply. Just keep in mind that every drop of breast milk that your baby gets is a gift and will give them a good healthy jump start to life.

After I had my hysterectomy at age twenty-six, we thought about adopting and surrogacy. I knew that I would need to breastfeed to bond with that child. That may not be true for everyone, but knowing you have options can itself be healing.

I also have induced lactation for lesbian families who both desire to breastfeed their child. It has been so beautiful to see both mothers able to care for and bond with their child, not to mention super convenient for being able to take turns. I think every tired breastfeeding mom who has had to wake up every three hours wishes this was an option. Can I get an amen?

There are several options for women who desire to breastfeed their adopted or surrogate-born infants. Most likely some amount of supplementation will be needed with any method. Building a milk supply takes time, and our main goal is to feed the baby. Eventually, you may be able to stimulate enough of a milk supply to solely feed your baby on expressed breast milk, but in the meantime, every little bit helps. Here is a list of the options you have for stimulating milk flow:

1. HORMONE STIMULANT WITH PUMPING: Hormonal stimulation with birth control pills to

stimulate growth and development of the alveoli (breast tissue) and milk ducts is the first step to inducing lactation. Taking the pills for a minimum of two months prior to breast stimulation is recommended, but the longer you take the hormones the better. There are several different brands of birth control that can be used. YAZ used to be the birth control of choice since the hormone combination worked best for stimulation of the pituitary gland, but due to severe side effects, your health care provider may recommend another option. Birth control combined with the use of a prolactin stimulant medication such as domperidone (motillium) or metoclopramide (Reglan) and breast pumping is recommended for the best results. **Reglan, however, is contraindicated for mothers with a history of depression, as this medication can increase feelings of anxiety and nervousness. I personally recommend domperidone, if you are able to get a prescription for it.

- Birth control should be taken continuously without the weeklong sugar pills. The hormonal stimulation, which has made the body think it is pregnant, is usually stopped about six to eight weeks before the infant's birth to trick the body into thinking it gave birth. At this time, breast pumping is initiated. Make sure you are sized for a correct fitting flange.

You most likely will need a smaller flange than what comes with the pump. The mother will gradually increase the time and frequency of each pumping session as well as the strength of the pump. It is vital that the mother use a good hospital-grade, double-electric stimulation pump such as the Medela Symphony pump, which has the capability to mimic the rhythm of a baby's suck ratio. It is recommended to pump both breasts simultaneously for fifteen minutes every three hours. The automatic cycling of the breast pump will provide your breasts with stimulation that is as similar to a baby's natural suck as possible.

- After the baby is born, place the baby skin to skin immediately. As soon as breastfeeding can be initiated, place the baby at the breast and use previously expressed milk or formula as a supplement. The use of a dropper or supplemental nursing system (SNS) is best. An SNS is a tube taped in place at the nipple that will allow the baby to get milk from a bottle while

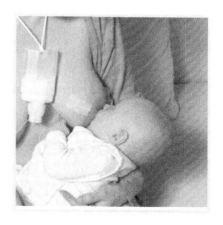

Medela supplemental nursing system

208

breastfeeding. Your lactation consultant can help you get started.

- After each nursing session, the mother should continue to pump for fifteen minutes. A three-step protocol will most likely be put into place: 1) breastfeed baby for fifteen minutes on each breast 2) supplement baby via SNS or bottle 3) pump for an additional fifteen minutes. This process usually lasts for at least two weeks or until a good milk supply has been initiated.

- It is usually necessary for the mother to continue using the prolactin stimulant for the entire duration of the lactation experience. It may be recommended to include herbal therapies. I am partial to moringa and all of the Legendairy Milk products, specifically those with goat's rue.

2. PROLACTIN STIMULATION WITH MEDICATION AND PUMPING: This is a non-hormonal method using only prolactin stimulants, such as the medication domperidone (motillium), and breast pump stimulation. The mother would begin the same procedures as listed above minus the use of birth control hormones. Instead, the mother would begin taking the prolactin medication six to eight weeks prior to delivery and begin pumping right away. Domperidone is the safest medication option for both

mom and baby for stimulating or increasing breast milk production (see earlier discussion about domperidone vs Reglan). The AAP (American Academy of Pediatrics) does promote and has approved the use of domperidone/motillium for increasing milk in breastfeeding mothers and has said it is safe for their infants. However, because the FDA has not approved it for this purpose, it can only be purchased via an online pharmacy: http:// inhousepharmacy.biz .

If you don't have a six to eight week window before the baby arrives, you can begin to pump as soon as the baby is born. Supplementing at the breast with a feeding tube would be initiated until the adopted mother began to see some milk flow from the breast. Use a good galactagogue such as Liquid Gold from Legendairy Milk, which has an added herb known as goat's rue that naturally stimulates additional breast tissue and ducts. Beginning this along with the pumping regimen is highly recommended.

3.BREAST PUMP ONLY: This would be the option for mothers who do not want to use any form of medication for stimulating growth. This would really only work for mothers who have breastfed previous children. The breasts have cellular memory, so therefore the pumping would awaken the breast tissue and allow the breasts to hopefully begin producing again. If the mother has never breastfed or been pregnant before, this is probably not the best option.

How much breast milk you produce depends again on whether you have been pregnant or breastfed before, the frequency and effectiveness of breast stimulation by both the infant and the pump, and the use of hand expression and breast massage prior to stimulation. Other factors will be your own hormonal response to the stimulation, as well as the infant's willingness to suckle at the breast.

In any case, it is important to nurse your baby as soon as possible after it is born. The baby will use the breast for comfort initially, but will eventually associate the breast with nutrition too. The more the baby is skin to skin and at the "breastaurant," the better chance that your breasts will produce more milk. Breast tissue always work by supply and demand. Allow the baby to use you as a stimulation for comfort. Nurse before, after, and between other feedings for as long as you and the baby are willing. Be sure to feed your baby eight to twelve times in a twenty-four-hour period. As your milk supply increases, the amount of milk you supplement with can be decreased. It may be helpful to keep a log of the number and length of each breastfeeding and pumping session, how much formula was given as a supplement, and how many wet and dirty diapers your baby is producing. Keeping a record will allow you to see just how much your baby is actually getting.

Keep in mind every woman is different. The most important thing to focus on is the physical contact and emotional bonds you are creating rather than the amount of milk that is being produced. Every drop of breastmilk your baby receives is a valuable. Before using any prescription or herbal medication, it is ALWAYS recommended that you consult your health care provider first.

Chapter 12: Breastfeeding, Birth Control, and SEX

Just because you have a baby does not mean that the romance has to die, though having a newborn in the house is going to make for some interesting romantic moments. I guarantee as soon as things begin to heat up, a baby is going to cry. It is just part of adjusting to life with a newborn. You have to keep your sense of humor when you go back to that phase of your relationship, be a bit more creative, if you will. Some couples are just too exhausted at this moment to even think about sex, let alone be creative, but I assure you that this too shall pass. Before you know it, you and your partner will be just as amorous as before.

There are a few things you have to consider when you resume your sexual lifestyle, now that you have just recently given birth and are breastfeeding. I am going to lay it all out for you. Consider it advice from the sisterhood.

First things first....there is a reason that your doctor has said no sex for the first six weeks after birth. For one, I'm sure having anything remotely close to your nether regions is the furthest thing from your mind right now. There is some

213

physical mending that has to take place regardless of if you had a vaginal birth or cesarean. If you had a vaginal birth, you are probably a bit stretched out at the moment, and you have some microscopic abrasions that need to heal. Don't worry, I promise you will go back to your normal vaginal size. (That was my husband's first question to our doctor...really?!?) After all, the vagina is a mucus membrane. But it takes some time for that to happen. If you had any form of tearing or an episiotomy, it may take a bit longer than six weeks to be ready to jump back in that saddle. Lube will become your best friend!

Second, your body is in a time of transition, and some women are extremely fertile. The lochia you are experiencing (this is the six weeks of bleeding that follows after birth) is different than a period, meaning you CAN ovulate during this time and you CAN get pregnant. (This is less likely if you are breastfeeding.) I can't tell you how many women go in for their six week check-up and find out they're pregnant again! So unless you really wanted "Irish Twins," I would wait a bit longer before hanging the figurative tie on the door handle. I once knew of a momma who got pregnant while recovering in the hospital. Did your jaw just drop to the floor like mine did? I mean, I know the hospital rooms are nice and private, but it isn't the Ritz Carlton, and her lady bits are freaking sore! I couldn't believe it when she told me, poor thing. Definitely not the news she was expecting at her doctor's appointment.

BIRTH CONTROL OPTIONS

At your six-week check-up, your doctor will discuss with you birth control options. There are many different methods of birth control that work well for the breastfeeding mother. Some women assume that breastfeeding alone is the perfect foolproof method of birth control. That isn't necessarily the case, and I always recommend using a barrier method such as condoms in conjunction with breastfeeding. Yes, it is true that lactating women will most likely not get their period for several months after the birth of their baby. This is because the lactation hormones suppress ovulation. However, for breastfeeding to truly be an effective form of birth control (this is known as LAM or lactational amenorrhea method), the mother has to be exclusively breastfeeding, never use a breast pump, and never offer a bottle. The breasts have to be stimulated by a baby ten to twelve times in a twenty-four-hour period for it to be successful.

The pump stimulates the breast differently than the baby's mouth, providing different hormone responses, which is why it can interfere with the LAM method of birth control. A baby will always stimulate a breast, and empty a breast, far better than the pump ever will. This isn't to say that if you use a breast pump you will resume menstruation sooner. Most likely, you will still not receive your period, but that does not mean your body can't ovulate.

As a matter of fact, there is something called the three-month dump that often occurs around the twelve-week marker. This is when your hormones shift and your milk supply dips temporarily due to the increase in estrogen. The three-month dump always seems to coincide with a growth spurt and can be incredibly frustrating for both mom and babe. This estrogen surge also will interfere with the flow and flavor of the breastmilk. Generally breast milk is sweet, like the leftover milk after you've eaten a bowl of Frosted Flakes. When your hormones shift, the milk becomes bitter...more like lemonade. Not bad tasting, just different. The baby may become fussy at the breast and go on a bit of a nursing strike to protest the change. If you had sugar your whole life and then took a sip of lemonade out of the blue, expecting sweet cream, you would react shocked also. Additionally, when you ovulate, your flow decreases and your milk ejection reflex takes longer. All this equals a cranky baby and irritated momma.

If you suspect that your period is a-brewing, the best thing to do to counteract the change is to add in some calcium/magnesium supplements. Take 500 mg when you ovulate (you will often be able to tell from the increase in vaginal discharge, which should be white, odorless, and sticky. If it smells weird or is an odd color, call your OB/GYN to make sure it isn't an infection) and also the week of your period. Some moms prefer to just take it every day as a precaution.

But remember, just because you are ovulating does not mean you will get your period. That feisty egg could linger for a while.

LAM METHOD

Scientific research has shown that women can effectively use the LAM method or breastfeeding method of birth control if they meet these three criteria:

1. The woman has not begun her menstrual cycle since the birth of her baby (lochia and spotting aside)

2. The mother is feeding her baby on demand and exclusively, day and night, without offering any other foods or liquids via bottle, and has not begun using a breast pump.

3. Her baby is less than six months old. At six months, the baby will be introduced to solids, thus resulting in fewer breastfeeding sessions and less breast stimulation.

Use of LAM method gives you a 2% chance of getting pregnant. However, if any one of these criteria changes, you are playing Russian roulette, and it is strongly recommended that you use another form of birth control.

217

CONDOMS/DIAPHRAGM/SPERMICIDE

Some families prefer to use a barrier method, such as a condom or diaphragm. This is obviously the safest method for your milk supply. Spermicides are safe, as very little will be absorbed and passed into your milk supply. However, they can be irritating to the vaginal lining.

According to naturalcycles.com, a popular and holistic approach to diaphragms and spermicide as used by many women in the past is sponges soaked in lemon juice to prevent pregnancy. The citric acid in lemons supposedly acts as a natural spermicide. The lemon rind itself (with pulp and juice removed) could also be inserted into the vagina and used as a cervical cap. Ummm...I do not recommend this at all! First of all, it isn't comfy. Second, lemon juice in the vagina sounds painful. And third, how in the actual hell would you not get a UTI. What I am trying to say is that just because it is natural does not make it the best choice over all. Before inserting anything into your vagina, consult with your doctor.

THE MINI PILL

One of the more effective birth control methods is a progesterone-only pill, also known as the mini pill. The medication itself is safe to pass into breast milk, but I strongly urge you to consider whether this method is best for you, as the progesterone hormone will affect your milk supply. Many mothers report a significant decrease in their supply once they begin taking any form of birth control pills, including the mini pill.

For some your supply may never be effected, but for majority of you who will experience a decrease, it is important to understand the need for extra stimulation and herbal therapy. Your supply may not recover completely, but with work it can return to some degree. If you feel that this is the best method for your family, despite the risk, then I do recommend taking a good herbal galactagogue such as the products from www.legendairymilk.com.

Regular strength birth control pills can have an effect on the volume and taste of the breast milk, as estrogen counteracts milk-making hormones, which is one reason why it is recommended to use a progesterone-only pill while lactating. It can be a crucial step in drying up your supply, however, when the time comes.

IUD

IUD, or intrauterine devices, are gaining popularity and are a rather effective method of birth control. There are five brands approved for use by the FDA: Mirena, Skyla, Paraguard, Liletta, and Kyleena. So what is an IUD and is it safe for breastfeeding? Depends on the brand, my friend.

An IUD is a small, T-shaped contraption made from polyethylene and manually placed in your uterus by your doctor in a standard office/outpatient visit. Typically, a string is attached, similar to that on a tampon. This allows the doctor to remove it should pregnancy be desired and gives you peace of mind that it is still in place each month. If you have an autoimmune disorder, I do not recommend using an IUD, as your antibodies may not agree with the polyethylene and attack the device, causing pain.

An IUD can last and protect against pregnancy for three to five years, depending on the brand. Mirena, Skyla, Liletta, and Kyleena secrete time-released hormones to prevent pregnancy and have the most effect on breastfeeding, specifically in the first month after insertion, as the hormone release is highest the first twenty-five days. They work by making you ovulate less, thickening cervical mucus to prevent sperm from entering, and preventing sperm from binding to the egg and attaching to the uterus.

ParaGard contains copper and does not release hormones, therefore it is the safest for lactating mommas. However, it works by creating an inflammatory response in the uterus, making it difficult for sperm to survive and an egg to attach to the uterus. In my opinion, anything that creates an inflammatory response will cause your body's immune system to react and can cause pain. Again, this is not a method I would choose if you have a history of chronic inflammation or autoimmune disorders.

Choosing a birth control option that is best for you should be a discussion had with your partner. Weigh the pros and cons of each option and, as always, before starting anything new, discuss your birth control options with your doctor to find the best fit for your family.

ADVICE FROM THE SISTERHOOD

There are a few extra things women should know about sex and breastfeeding that may come as a bit of a surprise but will certainly play a vital role in your lovemaking! Staying hydrated is very important to all breastfeeding mothers, as it helps with milk production and all around well-being. However, when a woman is lactating, all of her extra fluids go to making milk. Therefore, she will be drier than a desert storm down in her vagina during sex. I recommend using a lubricant such as Astroglide, YES lubricant (my personal favorite), KY Jelly, or whatever product works best for you. You will be happy, your partner will be happy, but most importantly your vagina will be very appreciative!

Oxytocin, also known as the "love hormone," is quite possibly one of the most important hormones in a woman's body. It is what is released to start contractions in labor, and it is also the hormone that is released with nipple stimulation to signal the body's milk ejection reflex. However, more importantly it is the hormone that is released when a woman experiences an orgasm. Needless to say, it is a VERY important hormone.

The milk ejection reflex is a rather strong reflex. When a woman's milk lets down, it doesn't just trickle out from the breast. It sprays out like a shower head! During sex, when you have an orgasm or your nipples are stimulated, your milk will let down and may spray in places you weren't expecting. Unless you want to give your partner a milk bath, I would wear a bra during intercourse! I had a woman describe it as her orgasm fountain. Just the sisterhood saving you from a potentially embarrassing moment in your relationship!

Do not get discouraged if it takes time for things to heat back up. Your body has been through a war. It's a beautiful war, but drastic changes have happened, nonetheless. You may not be feeling sexy. You may feel as if you are "fluffy" in places you weren't before. Your breasts are now no longer used just for sex; they have a very important purpose.

It is completely normal to not be interested in sex for a while. You probably feel "touched out" and your body probably hasn't felt like your own in months, maybe even years. When you are feeding round the clock, chasing toddlers, and constantly leaking, the last thing you may want is your partner all over you. However, they have undergone a significant change as well. It is a normal response for your partner to feel "neglected" or "replaced" by the baby. All your physical energy, touch, and affection has gone to this new little person. It is probably very confusing for both of you. You want to feel closer to your partner, but you also feel turned off by having to share your body with one more person. You may feel guilty for not being able to provide that specific need to your significant other, but you also need understanding from them that currently your body isn't your own. You need time and space.

All of this is perfectly normal and okay. If you communicate your concerns and feelings openly, it will prevent you both from feeling slighted in the relationship. You both are tired, and neither of you are mind readers. You have to talk and share constantly. I learned this the hard way. This is also a perfect time to not involve outside opinions in what works best for your relationship. The only two people that should have an opinion is you both. It takes humor, understanding, and time.

Reviving your sex life is key to sustaining a strong relationship bond with each other. But sex comes in all forms and fashions. When you two are communicating well and are connected well, you will work more as a team and be better parents as a result. So keep a sense of humor, talk things out with your partner, and most importantly have fun with each other. Parenting can be a difficult journey, but it shouldn't put a damper on some of the more exciting moments in your life. Enjoy each moment, and take it one happy step at a time!

Chapter 13: When Survivors Breastfeed

*** Trigger Warning: In this chapter I will be discussing various types of abuse, including sexual assault ***

This may be the most difficult chapter I write in this book, but it may also be the most powerful. I circled around this topic for weeks before I sat down to finally share my story. I want you to hear me when I say I understand what it is like to find out you are pregnant, be excited about motherhood, yet petrified at the same time that your past will create a barrier between what is natural and what is still healing. This is something that hits way too close to home for me, but has also strengthened me into the practitioner, mother, and advocate I have become.

When I was sixteen, my brother was my hero. We never fought. We went on adventures, and he taught me how to drive, how to draw, and how to dance. He made me laugh harder than anyone I ever met. He was eight years older than me and a raging alcoholic. We were living in Vegas at the time. My bedroom was on one end of the house, and my parents' was on the other. His room was next to mine. I distinctly remember earlier in the evening of January 15, 1996, getting ready for a date and him helping me pick out what I should wear to impress my boyfriend. Thinking about it now makes me sick, but I was young and naive.

At around 3:40 in the morning, I awoke to him barging into my room, completely drunk. He had drunk a pint of vodka, a pint of gin, and a six-pack of beer. Drunk was an understatement. He was mad at my dad about something, and knew that I was my dad's pride and joy. (Dad made it quite clear to all my siblings that I was his favorite, as I was his only biological child. Kind of sucked, to be honest.) Anyway, to my horror, my brother started yelling at me, not making any sense, hitting me, pushing me, holding me down. I will spare you the details, but he sexually assaulted me. I remember screaming, hoping my parents would hear me, but they didn't. I ran to their room, pounded on the door, and after about ten minutes, they eventually let me in. They had taken sleeping pills and were not really understanding what was going on. Most of it was a complete blur, and I was in complete shock.

The next morning, I tried to explain what happened to my parents, but they didn't want to hear it, and my father made it about him. It was never about him. I still do not know if it was more of the fact that my parents didn't want to accept that this happened to their daughter or the fact that their son was capable of such horrific things.

After about two weeks, my grandmother, who lived with us, sat me down and told me it had been long enough with the dramatics, I needed to get over it. That conversation still haunts me. My family acted as if nothing happened and went about their normal business. I was never the same. I still do not know if they believed me or not, and they still continued to try to push him into my life, but after years of therapy I realized that the betrayal from them not being there for me was worse than anything. It wasn't until after becoming a parent that I realized the denial and lack of compassion from my parents was more detrimental to me than the assault. These were people that were supposed to support me and protect me no matter what. It imprinted a painful message onto my soul.

Fast-forward five years, and I was pregnant with my first child. I was thrilled because I had always wanted to be a mother, and couldn't wait to hold this sweet one. It was all I ever dreamed of. But as soon as my belly grew and I felt the baby kick, I began to panic. My husband did not want to know what we were having—he really wanted that surprise moment of it's a ...—but the planner in me, and the survivor in me, needed something different. I did not understand why I was so terrified of having a boy. Why, as my pregnancy went on, I became more and more nervous. I had preterm labor at twenty-seven weeks and was put on complete bed rest. This of course gave me plenty of time to overthink everything. Hormones and trauma do not mix well, especially when you are a type A control freak like myself. I now know that there is also a significant link between sexual assault and preterm and prodromal labor.

The body keeps score, even if your memory does not. As my pregnancy progressed, and the vaginal exams grew more frequent, I found myself feeling less in control of my body and what was to come. I had a female doctor who was a dear friend of mine, who understood my history, but she too was pregnant with twins and ended up also going out on bedrest.

If I was going to have another doctor see me, I wanted it to be whomever was going to deliver my doctor's babies. Doctors of doctors have to be good, and she then would be able to book my appointments with her appointments so she could still follow me. The only thing was that this other doctor was a male, and that only made things worse.

This is why I am such a huge advocate of consent. He was amazing and did a great job, but he never asked me prior to an exam if I was ready. To him it was a routine part of the visit, and I should be prepared. Most doctors do not stop and ask permission to touch. They assume women understand it is part of the job description. I wish there was some way to convince healthcare providers that each time they touch a patient, they have to consider the idea, that what you may think is routine and normal, is foreign and sacred to the birthing mother. Taking a moment to ask permission to touch may make all the difference in the outcome of the birth and formation of those first moments of motherhood.

In pregnancy, I realized that I needed to know everything that was happening to me. I had to find out the sex of the baby. I needed to prepare—mentally, physically, and emotionally—if I was going to be giving birth to a boy.

To some of you this may seem odd, and I felt ridiculous being scared of my own baby. I thought I was super weird. However, the thought of a male developing inside me was difficult and left me feeling very empty. I kept everything to myself, not vocalizing my fears for months. (I do not recommend that, by the way.) After several weeks, my doctor realized something was off. We had a chat and decided it would be best for me to know the gender. When I found out I was carrying a girl, I felt a huge sense of relief. I knew I still had a lot of processing to do, but at least I could begin to move forward. Alyssa was born and changed everything about me. I was transformed. Breastfeeding was manageable and magical.

Fast-forward sixteen more months and I was four months preggos with baby number two. Same thing happened as before. I started to show, I felt the baby kick, and panic set in. Not only did the same fears surface about giving birth to a boy and having to breastfeed a boy, but now there was the potential of a brother/sister combo happening.

After my assault—which I had not dealt with because my parents had recommended I just ignore it—I had a hard time understanding how a healthy brother/sister relationship could exist. The fears came flooding back, but this time only stronger. So much was out of my control. How could I protect Alyssa and make sure that this child would stay safe and not turn into a monster that would hurt his sister? How was I ever going to be comfortable breastfeeding a boy? The idea of a male mouth on my nipple was traumatizing to me. Thankfully, God knew what I could handle (which is a hell of a lot, I have found out over the years) and gave me another girl. Sisters I understood. Sisters were safe. However, I needed to process this sooner or later to completely heal…and at that time later sounded glorious. I discovered this to be a mistake, as my postpartum depression was horrendous (I will share that story in the next chapter).

I found that therapy was a must. I had no idea that burying my trauma as I did, without dealing with it, would continue to traumatize me throughout my life, but it did. It wasn't until my girls were teenagers that I actually took the time and did the work. Mommas…let me tell you, if I could go back and heal sooner, I would. You are worthy enough to be a mother and worthy enough to heal yourselves.

My husband still wanted to be surprised about the gender of the baby, but I knew I had to find out and somehow convinced him that lavender was a neutral color. Not sure how I managed that one…but, hey, the heart hears what the heart wants. He truly was shocked when out came Alaina, as he was convinced I was having a boy, but in all the best ways. He loves being a dad to girls.

My doula had recommended a book to me by the incredible Penny Simkin, PT, called *When Survivors Give Birth*. It was probably the single most valuable book I had ever read. It made me realize that I was not the only one having these fears or thoughts. I was not weird! My fears were real and validated, and understanding the root of them gave me permission to heal.

According to national statistics reported at www.rainn.org, an American is assaulted every sixty-eight seconds. Every nine minutes the victim is a child. This means that one out of six people in the United States is a survivor, 90% female and 10% male. Worldwide that number jumps up to one out of three people who have been sexually assaulted in some form, and that is just those that are reported. Although the majority of survivors are women, it is important to be sensitive to the soon-to-be dads who are among the 10%. It is incredibly scary for them as well, especially if they have daughters. However, because this book is about breastfeeding, I am going to focus on women.

I have talked a lot about how birth can impact your breastfeeding journey. If you have the ability to hire a doula to help you with the birth process, and allow you to have some control in a very out-of-control situation, I recommend it. It will allow you and your subconscience to breathe a bit easier through the process. Even having a postpartum doula may make a difference in your first few days. Make sure you have communication with all birth workers—your nurse, doctors, IBCLC—and especially your partner. If there is fear, that will create tension, which ultimately will affect your supply.

When I meet with a new mother, I make it a priority to allow her the space to share with me any aspect of her story. Often, I can sense if there is a history of abuse, or if she is in an abusive relationship at home with her partner. I am hypersensitive to the signs, but, regardless, trust must be developed. I make it a point to get down on her level, ask permission before touching anywhere, allow time for questions, and of course allow the opportunity to process and grieve. Let me be the first to say, and I hope you hear me, that if the idea of breastfeeding is too hard, it is okay not to have the baby at the breast. Remember you have to do what is going to make you the best mom for your baby. There are, however, alternatives that allow you to still give your baby breastmilk. Pumping and bottle-feeding is a great option, or using a nipple shield. For some mothers, having a piece of plastic between the baby's mouth and the breast mentally allows her to feel safe and in control while offering the benefits of breastmilk.

Childbirth, breastfeeding, and parenting can be extremely difficult for someone who has a history of abuse. In my case, and in the case of several women I have stood by and supported, it takes work and major understanding to discover a path to healing. Hear me when I say the cycle can be broken. History does not have to repeat itself, and you are not alone is this frightening journey you may find yourself in. None of this is your fault. When your body is going through things you have absolutely no control over, that can be traumatizing in itself. Find a support system to walk you through, to help you set up boundaries and communicate what you need. It takes patience and love, but you are stronger than you think. You have been rebuilt, and you are a survivor, a warrior, and a mother. There is nothing more powerful than that.

Chapter 14: Baby Blues, D-Mer, PPD, Oh My

It would be remiss of me if I did not talk about the emotional side of breastfeeding and motherhood, because Lordy is it a doozy! I don't think that anyone is quite prepared for the emotional roller coaster that comes with the postpartum period, especially in those first few weeks. Who am I kidding? Worrying is part of motherhood! Thanks to Prozac and Jesus—it is the only way I get through life.

One thing I always stress with new moms is that the mental challenge is a physical change that results in an emotional manifestation. One morning you will wake up and it will hit you like a ton of bricks. Your hormones have been incredibly high throughout your pregnancy, and then—BOOM—you deliver a baby and a placenta, and your hormones, along with your dopamine and serotonin, take a nosedive. It is a physical change and definitely nothing to be ashamed of. It drives me bananas that there is a stigma wrapped around mental health and postpartum mood disturbances because I guarantee that most people will be faced with a form of depression at some point in their lives... including the men!

You may be wondering why I am spending time on the topic of PPD instead of writing more deeply about breastfeeding issues. My dear friend…these go hand in hand. So much of the postpartum mood is wrapped around lactation. We have to look at them side by side and make new mothers and their partners aware of the signs to look for. I was not so wise and thought I was invincible. If I'd only known then what I know now. The amount of sleepless anguish I put myself through because I thought I had to go through it alone is so heartbreaking. Parental anxiety is a fierce beast and if families are not given basic tools with evidence-based knowledge, that beast will take root and cause complete unrest.

My personal battle with postpartum depression was far worse with my second child, primarily because I now had two children under the age of two and never slept. I had no family around, my husband worked constantly, and since I was in the field of mother/baby, I was expected to have it all together. With my first baby, I had your standard weeklong baby blues. I remember a Taco Bell commercial coming on and, out of nowhere, I started sobbing, then laughing, because the little dog reminded me of the dog I had growing up, and I couldn't decide if I wanted a taco or a mexi-melt. What in the actual hell, Danielle?! I learned quickly to roll with the punches and to sleep when baby slept, and in time I felt the amazing bond I had prayed for. Now, don't get me wrong, I had many middle-of-the-night cry fests when I'd call my mom across the country at 2 a.m. and ask how I make the baby stop screaming. You know, normal new mom anxiety. With time, things became easier and I felt like I was in new mom bliss. However, when baby number two came...that all went to hell. To say I had PPD was an understatement.

There was a moment in particular that I remember like it was yesterday. It was the middle of the night when my baby must have been close to eight weeks. My toddler still wasn't sleeping through the night. I remember feeling so exhausted but being unable to fall asleep. It was this total brain fog insomnia that was never ending. I wanted to sleep, but no matter how hard I would try, I would just lay there for hours, wide eyed. There is a reason why sleep deprivation is used as a means of torture. My husband didn't know what to do with me anymore. As most men do, if they cannot "fix" the problem, they either dive into their own thing, work, or try to create a solution that looks more like being unsupportive (not his intention) than helpful. Every time she cried it was "she must be hungry" or "give her a bottle." He meant well, but I felt like I was failing...constantly. There was that maternal gaslighting again. The baby is crying and colicky, it must be my fault, what a bad mom I am. UGH, the lies I would tell myself! I knew deep down that wasn't true, but I was supposed to be the nurturing fixer of all things. I was the strong one!

One night in particular, I got up in the middle of the night, went downstairs into the bathroom where no one could hear me, and sobbed while painting the entire bathroom red (why red, I have no clue). I remember being scared to go into the kitchen because in that specific moment I wanted to die, and the kitchen is where the knives were. I just remember telling myself that if I kept busy, I wouldn't go there. "Just keep painting, Danielle, stay busy even if it is 3 a.m." I was in a dark place.

I thought that my kids would be better off without me as their mom, in the mental state that I was currently in. They deserved a mom who was whole and healthy, something I was not. I had grown up with a mother who battled chronic depression, anxiety, and bipolar disorder. Thankfully, I am not bipolar, but I was terrified of being "that mom" for my kids. So I began to listen to the lies in my head that I was better off dead, they were better off without me, and my husband would be just fine with someone else raising our babies. They didn't deserve to have a sad mom. I'd be doing them a favor if I was gone. They would be happier not being raised in a home full of depression and anger. Thankfully, my husband woke up (which I swear was the Holy Spirit looking out for me), and he came down to find me painting the walls and talking myself out of slitting my wrists. Yikes! It got dark, y'all. I hit rock bottom that night.

Looking back now, I wish I could just scoop up my frail, tired self and let her know it was going to be okay. My husband and I called the doctor the next day. He prescribed me an antidepressant and vitamin B complex, and I joined a support group for postpartum depression. I later found out that I was a carrier of the MTHFR gene, which explained A LOT! It was scary and humbling, but you know what? I found my people! I found a group of women who all felt the same exact way that I did. I wasn't alone in my thoughts or my feelings. What I found was hope. My husband saved my life that night, and my kids got their momma back. It took time and patience. It took not being afraid to take medicine because my brain at that moment was sick. It took a hell of a lot of love and a ton of gratitude.

There are four kinds of postpartum mood disturbances that I would like to break down: baby blues, postpartum depression, postpartum psychosis, and the often missed D-MER. It is important to remember that each of these disorders are completely independent of each other, yet often go hand in hand.

BABY BLUES happens in 50–80% of new mothers and usually starts on the second or third day after the birth. Symptoms may include crying spells, irritability, mood swings, sadness, fatigue, and a sense of loneliness. This may feel like defeat or an extreme sense of being letdown, as if this isn't what you had signed up for. And let's face it…the transition into parenthood is definitely hard to mentally prepare for. Although you love your baby, you will go through a period of grieving your past life. The baby blues is often associated with the hormonal flux that has happened post-delivery, which is why it elevates quickly once your hormones and dopamine levels normalize.

As bothersome as this can be, there are some things you can do to help as you wait for it to pass. As much as you possibly can, get rest. Easier said than done, I know. Sleep when the baby sleeps. You just gave birth—who cares about all the chores around the house right now? Your job is to take care of yourself and that amazing little human you created. Sleep and rest are going to get you back to normal faster than anything. If you need to stay in your pajamas all day until you have reached your eight hours of sleep then do it! Girl, you and your vagina/boobies have earned it. This is the time to allow other people to step in and care for you. (I am the WORST at this, so I know this is the pot calling the kettle black.) If people want to help you, LET THEM! Allow them to cook, clean, go grocery shopping, or hold the baby so you can take a nap and shower. Lean on your partner. They can't necessarily feed the baby, but they want to be in this with you. **You do not have to be everything to everyone!** Go back and read that last sentence again!

Make sure you are doing all you can to eat well and stay hydrated. Eating is usually the farthest thing from your mind at this time, but if you can remember to get small snacks in and drink to thirst, you will feel a world of difference. Seek out support from those around you that have been through it. We have many opportunities for support groups now both in person and virtually. You are not alone in this. Most importantly, trust yourself! God made you the momma of this little person for a reason. You have everything built within you to care for this sweet baby and for yourself.

POSTPARTUM DEPRESSION (PPD) is different than baby blues. Although it starts out the same, it often lasts longer, and the feelings are far more intense. Most of the time, the mother isn't even aware that she is going through it. Her partner will most likely notice it first. PPD occurs in about 10–20% of new mothers. It is a physical and psychological disorder comprised of biochemical, hormonal, and psychological factors. This can drastically affect your milk supply, which of course only makes things worse emotionally for momma, specifically if you are a first-time momma. Research has shown that, if left untreated, infants of mothers with PPD experience delayed psychomotor development and negative effects on their cognitive emotional growth.

I remember reading that back in the day and thinking, "Crap, my baby is only six weeks old, and I am already prepping them for therapy later in life!" Girl, that is not true. None of those are permanent. A delay is just a delay, which means they can catch up. Also, if you catch PPD in the early stages, most of that can be avoided.

Symptoms of PPD include:
- Inability to sleep despite severe exhaustion
- Anxiety/panic attacks

- Heightened concern or lack of concern for the baby
- Changes in appetite
- Low sex drive (also motherhood, just saying)
- Crying spells without cause
- Guilt, sadness, anger
- Despair or feelings of worthlessness
- Brain fog or forgetfulness
- Indecisiveness
- Diminished concentration
- Loss of interest in things you used to love
- Fear of harming the baby or yourself
- Obsessive/compulsive behavior

If any of the above symptoms sound familiar, contact your doctor or speak to someone you trust. PPD will not usually resolve in a few weeks or few months. If left untreated, it may lead to more panic attacks and anxiety. If caught early, PPD can be treated with medication, counseling, and support. I know better than anyone the fear surrounding the stigma of antidepressants. I wish that weren't the case, especially since more than half the world is taking them. If you had strep throat, you would take an antibiotic without blinking. Your mental health is the same. It may need medication to function correctly, and it most likely is temporary. Absolutely no shame in the getting-well game. PPD is a biochemical abnormality and does require the assistance of a physician.

Side note: **Postpartum Anxiety is often placed in the same category as PPD since they usually go hand in hand. However, it is possible, especially in first-time mothers, to notice only the anxiety aspect. Of course you will be anxious. You are trying to figure out how to care for this tiny human that you feel indescribably protective of, and you have never done that before. It is normal to question yourself about everything. It is when it turns into a compulsion that we have to pay attention. Statistically, there is an association between postpartum anxiety and reduced rates of breastfeeding and increased chance of supplementation with formula. If breastfeeding is super important to you, then it is crucial to pay attention to the warning signs and get the help you need.

POSTPARTUM PSYCHOSIS is quite different and quite rare, only affecting one to two new mothers per 1000. Personally, I have only encountered maybe three cases over my eighteen-year career. It may develop quickly or progress slowly. But it usually happens within the first few weeks postpartum. Symptoms include:
- Delusions
- Hallucinations
- Incoherence
- Thoughts of suicide
- Thought of harming the infant
- Irritability and mood swings
- Paranoia

• Hyperactivity

A woman who is experiencing any of these signs needs to find a capable adult willing to care for the baby and seek emergency care immediately. This requires immediate psychiatric intervention and often hospitalization. Again, this is rare and is a biochemical abnormality. Most women who develop psychosis have either a personal or family history of bipolar disorder or previous psychotic episode.

Research has shown that of the 2% of women who develop this disorder, 5% of them attempt suicide and 4% attempt infanticide. These women are experiencing a break from reality and are experiencing delusions and beliefs that feel real to them. They may have a religious meaning to them, and in their mental state these delusions make perfect sense. The majority of women who have psychosis do NOT harm themselves or their babies, but emergency close monitoring is needed since these delusions can lead to irrational decisions. This is absolutely treatable. It is extremely important that these women do not feel judged and understand that they are supported completely.

D-MER (DYSPHORIC MILK EJECTION REFLEX) is completely different then PPD or baby blues, as it ONLY happens during letdown with the milk ejection reflex. When oxytocin is released, it causes an intense rapid drop of dopamine. It can present differently in every woman, but they all have one common characteristic, which is a wave of negativity or melancholy prior to letdown.

This emotional response has been described as a feeling of dread or a pit in your stomach. The breastfeeding mother experiences this surge of negative emotions about thirty to ninety seconds prior to her milk letting down when breastfeeding or pumping or even with spontaneous letdown from simply hearing a baby cry. By the time the milk actually releases and the baby starts gulping, the feelings have dissipated. The surge of emotion is triggered by the sudden rush of oxytocin, causing a quick drop in dopamine, which can also happen when a woman orgasms, has nipple stimulation outside of lactation, or is going through menopause—it can happen anytime there is a rush of hormones. I experienced D-MER with both children and to this day, twenty years later, will have a wave of dread when I orgasm, which usually means I am low in B vitamins. It doesn't happen every time, but it does help me know when I am nutrient deprived. Probably TMI for you all, but I'm being real about my experiences.

Although mothers with D-MER sometimes express the emotions a bit differently, there are many similarities in the language that they use. Also, it is important to realize that the intensity of these emotions vary from person to person. The emotional responses experienced with D-MER seem to fall within three categories: despondency, anxiety, and agitation. Many mothers have described it as a hollow feeling in the stomach, anxiety, sadness, dread, introspectiveness, nervousness, anxiousness, emotional upset, angst, irritability, hopelessness, and general negative emotions. Man, can I relate with this one. For me, the most difficult part was knowing this was coming every time I lactated, which was easily ten times a day. This of course caused me to be anxious as I anticipated the attack. The good news is that D-MER usually goes away around the three-month marker. Some mothers may experience it the entire duration of their breastfeeding journey, but in those cases the severity drops significantly.

Weaning is not usually necessary, although if the feelings are too intense and it impedes your ability to be the best mom you can to your baby, then your supporting village needs to honor your decision to stop. The majority of the time, understanding that what you are feeling is a real, valid condition helps to encourage you along your journey. Knowing that there is an end in sight may also help you get to your breastfeeding goals.

In some cases, women will only feel the symptoms of D-MER while pumping or with spontaneous letdowns, but not when baby is at the breast. It is possible that this has to do with the oxytocin rush, which helps to counteract the negative feelings of dysphoria due to the baby being placed directly on your skin. It becomes more of a hormone wash.

There really is no way to predetermine if a woman will be prone to D-MER, as her medical or personal history does not directly affect this response. We do know that it is not related to a history of sexual abuse or traumatic birth, but if you have that in your past, you may feel reminiscent of an earlier time where you experienced these same feelings of dread. If you had an experience that caused the same dopamine drop to occur, it can make you revisit those moments.

So what in the world causes this? To be perfectly honest, I do not think anyone truly knows yet. All we know it that it is dopamine mediated, but no one knows why some mothers have it and some do not. I personally feel it is related to MTHFR, but that is just a theory I have. It would explain why D-MER is picky, and why, once you experienced this, you will have it with each baby. MTHFR makes letdown intense and causes a sensitivity to the normal drop in dopamine. This all could also just be related to a nutritional deficiency or a breakdown in hormones as the gal ages and matures. Could be a mutation of the dopamine receptor. Clearly, there is still more research needed, but in my personal practice I have seen a link between mothers who have MTHFR and this response. It is something I currently am doing a research study on, so I will keep you all posted on my findings.

There are a few things that you can do. I have found that adding in a vitamin B complex does help, as does adding omegas to your diet. Remember, if you do have MTHFR, you will need a methylated version of vitamin B-12. Since D-MER is not a form of depression, this should be a temporary issue. Thank goodness for that!

Although there are medications that can help balance out any one of the above disorders, which I 100% support, there are some natural remedies you can try as well. Depression is known to be linked to chronic, low-grade inflammation. Cortisol (the stress hormone) is an anti-inflammatory in the short term. But when you experience chronic stress, this effect diminishes, leaving you open to increased inflammation and higher risk of depression. Psychological stress can also trigger the release of cytokines, a broad category of small proteins and peptides. This too can lead to depression. While medications can help tremendously, some mothers feel more comfortable approaching this in a holistic way. Some options are:

- Blue light therapy
- Exercise (this may be the last thing you want to do when you are feeling down, but it does help)
- Vagal nerve stimulation
- Therapy and support groups
- Vitamin supplementation like omegas and B vitamins. I would avoid St. John's Wort, however. That is a commonly used herb and it will pop up on a Google search, but is not safe for breastfeeding. You should always seek the advice of a healthcare provider prior to the use of anything herbal.

- Diet—eating more fruits, veggies, whole grains, and specifically fish. Research has shown that low seafood consumption is associated with a sixty-five times higher lifetime risk of developing depression and fifty times higher chance for postpartum depression. People who eat a healthier diet have fewer mental health problems. Easier said than done, I know.

I mentioned earlier how any one of these mood disturbances can set you up for early weaning, primarily because of the lack of support and stigma wrapped around mental illness. Hear me again when I say:

You HAVE to do what makes you the best mom for your family, including what is best for your mental health. You have not failed, you have prevailed. Do not let anyone take away from you the warrior journey you have had. If breastfeeding is taking a toll on your mental health and your ability to feel whole, then the correct decision as a mother IS to stop. This does not make you a bad mom…this makes you a loving, responsible mom. Do not listen to the lies being told to you by society and yourself. You are strong! You are brave! Girl…you are a kick-ass momma, and I am so incredibly proud of you!

Chapter 15: Pump...Pump It Up! Now Get Back to Work

Let's be real, no one loves the pump. You love your baby, you don't love the machine. Most moms have a love/hate relationship with their motorized maternal milker, as my husband would call it. However, every mom needs some form of a breast pump, whether it is a manual or a super fancy, hands-free double electric. Maybe your boobies feel like they are about to explode and you are desperate to get every last drop out, or you are returning to work and need to store milk. You might be pumping to increase supply or simply just want a break from the baby and need to pump for some me time.

My breast pump was the very first thing that I purchased three days postpartum. I was not prepared twenty years ago, can you tell? I will say this, though—breast pumps have improved drastically over the years. Gone are the days of lying low in a bathroom stall because there was nowhere else to pump, strapping on the one-size-fits-all flange, and starting the ridiculously loud motorized process of expression. It sounded like the loudest bull horn vibrator back in my day. What a victory it was for women when the Affordable Care Act of 2010 supported the rights of breastfeeding/pumping mothers everywhere. Federal law now requires employers to provide reasonable break time for an employee to express breast milk for her nursing child for one year after the child's birth. This means at least two or three additional fifteen-minute pumping breaks outside of lunch hours.

Employers are also required to provide a place, other than a bathroom, that is shielded from view and free from intrusion from coworkers and the public. Thank the Lord! Chef's don't prepare meals in a bathroom, so mothers should not have to prepare their baby's meals in a dirty bathroom stall either. Before you return to work, make sure you and your employer are up to date with your state's maternity laws. Now is the time to start advocating for your family. If your employer refuses to comply, they can face fines of up to $50k. I think that is persuasive enough to get you a clean pumping plan.

Another amazing part of the Affordable Care Act was that insurance companies finally had to step up to cover the costs of breast pumps and lactation consults. Girl…take them up on that! There are several options of pumps for you to choose from, and it truly depends on preference. I would discuss with your IBCLC what she feels is best for your situation. Insurance coverage has changed the game for so many mothers seeking care. I cannot tell you how awesome it was to finally be able to offer free breastfeeding support to so many mothers. However, we have a long way to go in this department. While most insurance companies will reimburse for lactation care, they definitely do not make it easy. You would think that with all the science backing up the immunity and well-being benefits for both mother and baby, every insurance company would be jumping on the bandwagon. It would save so much money in the long run. Especially now with Covid and the amazing attributes breastmilk has when it comes to treating this stubborn virus.[10] Alas, this is not the case, but is a fight we keep on waging.

The United States is the only country that does not support solid maternity care, specifically in the postpartum period. We are requiring our mothers to return to work within six to eight weeks of giving birth, while their bodies are still recuperating from delivery, their hormones and sleep have yet to balance out, and their babies have yet to figure out any form of a routine. No wonder we have a higher incidence of postpartum depression in our country. Canada and Germany have it right —one full year of paid maternity care. Their PPD rates are significantly lower, and their breastfeeding success rate is drastically higher than here in the states. If you or your partner can take paid family leave, I would strongly suggest it. You will need this time. In the meantime, we will keep fighting for maternity rights.

There are many reasons why a woman will need to pump at some point in her breastfeeding journey. Understanding which pump to use and what schedule to pump on is very confusing. So let's break it down:

1. **Pumping to increase supply**

Your breasts work by supply and demand. Remember our old pal FIL? The milk is made the minute you pump or the baby latches on. So if you are pumping strictly to increase supply, the best route to go is to pump both breasts at the same time for ten minutes after a feed. You may not see much come out, but the point is to trick your body into thinking that there is a growth spurt happening, and therefore your breasts need to up their game. Typically, I recommend doing this at least three times a day, but you can do this after every feed if you so desire. I personally am not a fan of complicated plans because they wear the mother out and backfire. But three times a day does seem to make a significant difference, especially if done over a span of two weeks. Do not get discouraged if you do not see much milk come out. The goal of this is to increase supply, not to store milk. Think of it as an insurance plan for your boobies. I would actually be concerned if you pumped out several ounces directly after a feed. That would tell me that either the baby is not transferring the milk or that you may have an overproduction issue. As I mentioned earlier, if you are anxious about how much milk you are pumping out, place socks over the bottles. I know this may sound silly, but our minds are powerful. If you are pumping and staring at the bottles, your boobs are going to get performance anxiety! Just take deep breaths and think of your baby.

Another option to increase supply is power pumping. Basically, the mother pumps off and on for an hour. Start with a ten minute session, break for five minutes, then pump for five minutes, break for five minutes, etc., for sixty minutes. This is done once or twice a day. It does work, but it's not something I would do every day. I would power pump around the time of your period or ovulation, or anytime you notice a growth spurt. It is a quick fix for a drastic drop.

2. Pumping to relieve engorgement.

I talked quite a bit about engorgement in previous chapters. Whether it is because of onset of milk production, you finally slept through the night and baby missed a feed, or you happen to be making more milk than the baby can take in, you will end up engorged at some point. I mentioned earlier how ice and heat soaks help to alleviate the discomfort of engorgement, but we also have to get the milk out. Pumping and hand expressing is often the easiest way. I do recommend icing the breast first to bring down additional swelling. Also, shake the breasts in a clockwise motion towards the armpit for lymphatic drainage. It may be that you will need to pump one breast at a time so that you can wrap a warm, moist towel around the breast and use your hands to help massage. You can also do what we call third spacing or reverse pressure softening, which is initially pushing fluid out of the areola prior to attaching the flange.

I would only pump till the breast is softened. If you pump for too long, it will send a mixed message to the breast. As soon as you see the milk stop spraying, and your breast is less firm, then stop. This is usually no more than five or ten minutes. If no milk is flowing after one or two minutes, then stop, soak the breast in hot water, massage, and try again.

3. Pumping to store milk for work and/or free time

So many moms are concerned that if they pump, and then baby acts hungry directly after, they won't have enough milk, or they will take away from the baby's next feed. Let me reassure you, this is not the case! You are the factory. Just keep drinking your water and staying hydrated, and you will be just fine. Yet I know that all moms want reassurance that they can build a storage for when they return to work. So here is the best way to go about that.

Pick a time and designate that as your pumping-for-storage moment. The best time would be one hour after the start of the morning feed. For example, if you feed your baby at 7 a.m., drink a big glass of water and pump both breasts at 8 a.m. for fifteen minutes. Your body will begin to recognize that 8 a.m. pump session as its own feed and will begin to produce just as much at that time as you do any other time of the day. Drink another glass of water and have some oatmeal, and you will be fine for when baby is due to eat at 10 a.m. Consistency is key, however. Start this process about three weeks before you are set to return to work. It will give you a good head start for a nice freezer stash.

You can mix bottles of previously pumped milk with fresh milk if you want as long as it has been cooled first. According to updated CDC guidelines, mixing warm, freshly expressed breast milk with already cooled or frozen milk is not advised because it can rewarm the older stored milk, compromising the antibody component. It is best to cool freshly expressed milk before combining it with older, previously cooled or frozen milk. If you do this, you need to abide by the oldest pump date for storage. I recommend only freezing the amount needed for each feed. Once frozen milk is thawed, it has to be used that day. Also remember that the color and fat content will change from day to day, so do not worry if it looks different every time.

When pumping at work, or even at home, you do not have to wash out the pump pieces completely each time. You can place your flanges in a Ziplock bag in between pumping sessions and place in the refrigerator. This will keep everything sterile. When you are limited on time, this is a lifesaving hack! I also recommend pumping directly into bags instead of bottles if possible. Makes storage so much easier, especially when transporting home.

Below is an easy table to guide you on the correct protocol and guidelines to consider for breast milk storage.

FRESHLY EXPRESSED BREAST MILK
Room temperature (66–72 degrees F): 4 hours
Cooler with frozen ice packs (59 degrees F): 24 hours
Refrigerator (32–39 degrees F): 5–7 days

Self-contained freezer (below 32 degrees): 3–4 months

Deep freezer (0 degrees F): 6 months

Thawed breast milk that has been previously frozen can stay in a refrigerator for twenty-four hours only. It should never be stored in a cooler or at room temperature. It is also very important that you never refreeze thawed milk. It is best to store your expressed milk in two-ounce increments so that you don't waste any residual milk after a feed. You will find that your milk is like liquid gold, and you will hate to throw any of it away.

If your baby has only finished a portion of the bottle, it must be finished within two hours because saliva has entered and contaminated the milk. Use the unfinished milk in the baby's bath that evening. It does wonders for the skin and soothes rashes or eczema.

***Special note: Expressed milk will separate upon sitting. The fat and protein will float to the top, and the water will separate to the bottom. This does NOT mean the milk has curdled or gone bad. It is perfectly normal for the milk to do this. DO NOT THROW IT AWAY! Simply shake the milk after warming it. It will mix well and be perfectly fine to feed to the infant. I cannot begin to tell you how many times my husband threw away my milk, thinking it had spoiled! A little piece of me died each time. He quickly learned the dos and don'ts of breastmilk storage. There is some false information out there stating that if you shake breast milk instead of swirling or stirring it, the properties become damaged and break down. There is no scientific backing for this. So swirl, twirl, shake, stir to your heart's content.

Your milk can spoil, however, if it sits out too long without being properly stored. Rancid breast milk has a very sour smell and taste, just like how cow's milk does. If your expressed milk does not smell fresh but does not have that rancid, could-peel-paint-off-the-wall smell, it might not be spoiled. It may have to do with how the milk is being stored. It might be helpful to evaluate how you are storing your milk to see if you are doing it correctly.

1. Storage Containers: Use plastic or glass bottles that have been properly sterilized, or milk storage bags designed to protect the components of breast milk.

2. Correct Temperature: Make sure the temperature of the refrigerator and freezer are set correctly. Store the milk in the back of the fridge or freezer rather than in the door, where temperatures are typically warmer. Make sure your door closes, as sometimes this can lead to freezer burn and result in improper freezing. (If your fridge goes out or there is a power outage and your milk begins to thaw, it can be refrozen if there are still ice crystals in the milk and it is substantially cold.)

3. Keep It Sealed: If the storage container isn't sealed tightly, it can cause odors from other foods to seep in, interfering with the freshness of the milk. Try keeping

baking soda in your fridge to minimize unwanted smells.

If you still are having a problem with your milk not appearing fresh, it could be due to an overproduction of an enzyme called lipase that is naturally found in human milk and is responsible for the breakdown of the milk proteins. This tends to give the milk a "soapy" taste and consistency. The milk is still safe to feed, but the baby may not be as interested.

Lipase has several very beneficial dietary functions such as:

- Aids in keeping the milk fat emulsified (or mixed well) with the protein portion of the milk, known as the "whey."
- Keeps the fat globules tiny so that the body can easily digest them
- Helps to break down the milk fat, enabling the fat-soluble nutrients such as certain vitamins (A&D) and free fatty acids (responsible for protecting the baby's immunity) to be more easily absorbed by the body.

If there is an excess of lipase enzyme, then the fat gets broken down too quickly after being expressed and exposed to oxygen, thus resulting in the change. The milk is not harmful, and most babies are not bothered by the mild change. However, the longer the milk sits, the more apparent the taste/smell becomes, and the baby will likely have an aversion to it.

Once the milk has oxidized or become "soapy," there unfortunately is nothing you can do to reverse it to its previous state. However, there is something you can do to help prevent the bothersome change with future expressed milk. If you are certain that your milk storing issues are related to an excess of lipase, you can try scalding the milk prior to storing it in the freezer or fridge. Scalding the milk soon after it is expressed will stop the breakdown process of the fats that is caused by the excess enzymes. To scald, heat the milk in a pan on the stove to around 180 degrees F, or until you begin to see bubbles forming around the edge of the pan. DO NOT bring the milk to a rolling boil. Once the proper temperature has been reached, immediately cool the milk and store in an airtight container.

It is true that scalding the milk at such a high temperature will kill some of the antibodies and probiotic features of breast milk. But there are still many valuable components to breast milk that will still provide better nutrients to your baby then store-bought formula. As long as your baby is receiving breast milk directly from the source a couple times a day— and yes, mommas, that means you—losing the additional antibodies from the heat-treated milk shouldn't be a problem. Eating a diet high in omegas with good fats, such as nuts and avocados, can also help reduce the amount of fat getting broken down.

4. Exclusive pumping momma

I have to first give a massive shout-out to you moms who are exclusively pumping. It is a lot of work and takes dedication. It just shows what an awesome momma you are. Despite some difficulties with latching your baby, or difficulty in your supply, you are still doing everything in your power to give your sweet one breast milk. Do not let ANYONE tell you that pumping and bottle-feeding your milk is not breastfeeding. You absolutely are breastfeeding. It is just being delivered by a different route. You are still providing incredible nutrients and antibodies. Remember to periodically keep your baby skin to skin and, if possible, take some of the baby's saliva and allow it to absorb into your nipple. This will help your body recognize specifically what your kiddo needs.

When you are pumping to bottle, it is important that you have a properly fitted flange and that you are attempting to match the baby's feeding schedule. If baby is having a growth spurt, I would try to fit in a few more pumping sessions that week so that your body will catch on and produce more.

One perk to pumping to bottle is that you do have a bit more freedom since you are not the only one feeding. I would make sure that you are pumping every two to three hours in the day, and at least once in the evening, until baby begins to sleep through the night. Then I would mimic the baby's sleep

259

patterns. Pump both breasts for fifteen minutes each feeding session. Make sure you have comfortable flanges and always make sure you are taking sunflower lecithin. You will be more prone to clogs, and that will help prevent them.

TYPES OF PUMPS

Trying to figure out which pump to buy is like trying to find the perfect-fitting bra. There are so many options! They come in many colors, shapes, and styles. Some are comfortable and others hurt like crazy. And while most get the job done, none of them will ever fit perfectly. There are hands-free pumps, closed-system pumps, and open-system pumps. Each pump has various modes and flange inserts. The breast pump industry is booming and confusing! Picking the best pump boils down to your personal preference and what you will be using it for. Pumps are broken down into four different categories: hospital grade, double electric, battery operated, and manual. There are at least twelve different brands with various models and accessories. I am going to break it down to give some insight on what pump would fit you best.

HOSPITAL GRADE: These are double-electric closed-system pumps, meaning there is a barrier to prevent overflow of fluids into the pump system, specifically in small areas that cannot be sterilized. This is more hygienic and allows for multiple users. Typically, these pumps include computer technology to mimic the suck speed and rhythm of the newborn. It is designed primarily for the use of NICU moms who are separated from their baby, mothers of twins, and mothers with a history of delayed onset of milk production or previous breast reduction surgery. The Medela Symphony, Ameda Purely Yours, and Spectra Synergy are typically the most expensive and are only available through a hospital for renting.

ELECTRIC OPEN SYSTEM: These work very similar to a hospital-grade pump in regards to function, but they do not have the closed-system technology. This means there is no barrier between the milk and the motor, so milk flows through tubes and other small pieces into the bottle and may come into contact with the pump mechanism. These are significantly cheaper than a closed-system pump, but I highly recommend that you do not borrow a pump from anyone. Even if your aunt Judy's second cousin twice removed claims that she only used it once, don't take it. Your baby's immune system and yours are precious.

Most of the bottle companies also make pumps, but the research into these systems is not as advanced. It can be difficult to get milk to express or letdown easily because of how painful they can be due to suction levels and poor fitting flanges. You will have to change out various parts every six months due to wear and tear, and most pumps only have about a two-year shelf life before the motor quits on you. When choosing an electric pump, most moms defer to whatever their insurance company will provide them. Pumps are pricey, so taking the free one sent to you, whether it fits or not, is better than nothing.

BATTERY OPERATED HANDS-FREE: Hands-free pumping is gaining more and more popularity, specifically with working moms. It used to be that the only hands-free option was to strap your electric plug-in pump into a pumping bra, which always caused chafing. It wasn't ideal, but it allowed your hands to be free to do something other than holding bottles for twenty minutes. The modern hands-free pumps allow for discrete, quiet pumping while going about your workday. Depending on your job, this can be a lifesaver, especially if you are on your feet all day. The difficulty with these pumps is comfort and cost. These can range anywhere from $250 to $575, depending on whether insurance covers any portion. Flange sizing is important for adequate milk removal, and with these pumps you are limited with size. Most women have a love-hate relationship with these, and if you can find a way to pull it off without looking like Madonna, that is a win!

MANUAL PORTABLE HAND PUMPS: These come in handy for clogged ducts and on-the-go pumping. The Haaka, which I have mentioned in several chapters, is a must have for all breastfeeding moms. While your baby breastfeeds, you can place it on the other breast without needing to do anything. It is not designed for stimulation or to increase supply. The main purpose is to catch the milk that comes from multiple letdowns. Plus, it can help remove clogged ducts and milk blebs and treat sore nipples (when used with hot water and Epsom salt).

Medela and Avent do make hand pumps where you control the suction and motion. This is great for when you are out running errands and do not have time to pump or feed. The downside is that after five minutes of hand expressing, you get tired, which weakens the suction. In my opinion, these are more for a quick pump while driving or relieving some pressure if you are engorged and it is difficult for the baby to latch.

Because there are so many brands and models of breast pump, I decided to take it to the real expert, aka the pumping mom herself. I interviewed 100 moms to get their opinion on what type of pump they found most helpful. Here is what they had to say:

BRAND	MODEL	PRICE	DESCRIPTION
Spectra (Hospital grade)	S1 S2 Gold	$245 $191 $325	Blue, rechargeable Pink, plug in Multiple settings
Medela	Pump in Style Harmony Freestyle	$199 $30 $325	Double-electric dual-speed Single, manual pump Double-electric, portable
Willow	One style	$500	Hands-free, wearable
Elvie	One style	$549	Hands-free, wearable
Baby Buddha	Quiet Electric	$250	Double-electric, portable, lightweight

BRAND	MODEL	PRICE	DESCRIPTION
Hygeia	Single Pro	$20 Some insurance covers it 100%	Two-hand manual pump Double-electric, cordless
Ameda	Mya Joy Manual	$249 $33	Hospital grade, electric Single hand only
Motif Luna	One style	$189	Double electric, lightweight
Lansinoh	Signature Pro Smartpump 2.0 Manual	$85 $160 $24	Double-electric Double-electric, dual- speed Single-hand pump
Bella Baby	Double electric	$50	Portable, strong suction

BRAND	MODEL	PRICE	DESCRIPTION
Avent	Electric Natural motion	$269	Electric, motion technology
	manual	$45	Single-hand pump

The above guide is a reference of the eleven top brands and their prices in order of preference. Spectra was favored by 80%. Mothers stated that when it came to choosing the right pump, it often depended on if the pump was portable, had multiple compression modes with various speeds, and the ability to change out parts. I would agree that you want to find a pump that feels comfortable, yields milk, and has the ability to switch out parts if needed for smaller flanges, pump bags, and silicone inserts. It seems with the hands-free portable pumps, it boils down to personal fit. Elvie was more popular among our mommas than Willow, mainly due to discreetness.

I often get asked what my personal favorite is. I would choose Spectra or Medela, as they have done the most research into the technology behind milk expression. Hygeia is my least favorite. There is a reason it is the least expensive and that insurance companies can afford to give it out for free.

It is a knock-off Medela that does not seem to work well. I would stay away from this brand and focus on a pump that has the ability to mimic your baby's suck pattern.

A few tips about pumping that no one will tell you.

1. ALWAYS lubricate the flanges with coconut oil or nipple cream (not lanolin) prior to pumping. This will prevent friction and unnecessary pump trauma.

2. Get sized and fitted for a flange. Most of the time, the reason a pump doesn't empty the breast is because the mother is using the wrong size flange. When pumping, your nipple should not extend to the base of the tube, resulting in what we call elastic nipples. If this is happening, too much of your areola is being sucked in, which will result in nipple pain and areola damage. The majority of pumps come with a 24mm and 27mm flange made of hard plastic. I am finding that a smaller size is often needed, such as a 21mm or 19mm, most often a 17mm. They make them as small as 13mm. You may also find that your two breasts needs a different size. Totally normal. If you cannot find a size that fits you well, you can always get a *pumping pal*, which is a one-size-fits-all flange that is angled and will fit into any model pump.

3. As I've mentioned before, place socks over your bottles so you do not see the amount of milk you are

pumping out. Our mind is a powerful tool. If you are staring, milk will not flow.

4. The pump is not an accurate determiner of the amount of milk you are making. Statistically, the pump leaves behind about a half ounce in each breast. If you know you make more than you are pumping out, it may indicate the need for a new pump. Or there could be a mental block preventing expression. You may need to use warm compresses or vibration massage to help release milk.

When you return to work, there will be a transition period for both you and your baby. There will be some grief as you process the change and adapt to the new lifestyle. Embrace it, girl. This is the beginning of many changes to come and adjustments to make throughout your journey of motherhood. It is okay to feel sad. It is normal to experience mom guilt in this moment, but try not to listen to those lies. It is okay to have a life of your own. Will your supply take a hit? Possibly, but that is what Pump Princess by Legendairy Milk is for. If you need someone to walk you through the pumping process with a schedule, find an IBCLC that jives with your personality and way of thinking to write you out a schedule. This is temporary, my friend. Never forget your power and what a badass rockstar you are.

Chapter 16: Bottles, Nursing Strikes, Nipple Confusion?

One of the most frustrating things for a new mother who is getting ready to go back to work, or those who stay at home but simply want a break, is a baby who simply will not take a bottle. Most mothers have the opposite problem—the baby wants to ONLY take the bottle and not the breast—which can be a sign of another problem, such as a tongue tie. However, you would be surprised how many babies there are that simply refuse any bottle, of any kind.

Now you may think that is flattering. After all, your baby adores you so much that he wants nothing else but the comfort of your breast. I agree this is beautiful and makes mom feel like a million bucks most of the time. But even she needs to have a moment to breathe.

All new moms agree that while breastfeeding is a natural, beautiful thing, sometimes momma just wants a moment to herself, something that you ABSOLUTELY deserve! Motherhood is great, but you need your alone time too, and a little private time with your partner as well. Date night? What is that? When I was a new mom, the thought of heading out to the store for one whole glorious hour seemed like heaven…

even if it was just to the pharmacy. But if you have a baby that absolutely refuses to take a bottle…this is super stressful. You feel stuck, trapped, and sometimes alone. All the pressure to feed is placed solely on you.

If you are getting ready to go back to work, the stress of a baby not taking a bottle skyrockets. You are on a time crunch, and baby just isn't having it! Stress levels rise, your milk supply hits its demise, tears start flowing, and it is a hot mess of chaos. So let's avoid that, shall we? Here are some great tips to help your little bundle of joy take that first bottle!

Step 1: Find the right bottle, which can be an expensive trial-and-error scenario. However, you want to find the bottle that is going to be most similar to the breast. In my opinion, there is no such thing as nipple confusion; there is just flow preference. If the baby has normal functioning oral anatomy and is positioned correctly either at the breast or bottle, the baby should have no difficulty transferring milk, and no problem going back and forth between the two methods. The problem arises

Pace feeding with Lansinoh bottle

when the flow of the bottle differs from the flow of the breast. This is why paced bottle feeding (videos available on my Instagram) and reclined biological feeding are recommended. If the baby is rejecting the bottle and gagging, the first step should be finding out if the baby is tied. Next you want to get a wide-mouth bottle. The brands I prefer are Lansinoh and Breastflow because the nipples extend and compress very similar to that of the breast. If those are not an option, my follow up brands are Playtex Nurser, Avent, and Kinde. Again, your baby will have a preference, and it doesn't really matter which bottle you use, just as long as it is a silicone wide-mouthed bottle with a slow-flow nipple. The flow must mimic that of mom. Start with one and offer it at least seven times in a row. If it doesn't work, then move on to the next.

Step 2: Someone other than mom needs to give that first bottle. If mom is the one to offer the bottle, the little one is going to smell the milk on mom and want the "breastaurant" versus a bottle. So have dad, grandma, auntie, anyone else that is not mom give that first bottle. This is an excellent time for momma to leave the room, go get a pedicure, or, hey, even take that much needed and desired shower. 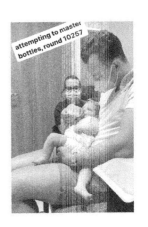 This is a great way for dad or grandma to bond. Regardless…mom needs to leave. If the baby can smell her, see her, or even hear her, he won't participate as easily.

Step 3: Make sure you are feeding the baby in a position that is breastfeeding friendly. There are two ways to go about this. First you can place baby on his side with the bottle horizontal. This mimics the breastfeeding position and allows for the use of acupressure points for calming. Make sure that you tilt the bottle so there is enough milk in the nipple without any air. In the above picture, you can see how all three of the feeding pressure points are being used. Only fill the bottle with 2 to 3 ounces of expressed breast milk or, if not available, pediatrician-recommended formula to start. It's always best to start with too little rather than too much milk. Once baby has fed from the bottle, you MUST discard any remaining milk. Saliva will transfer via the bottle nipple, beginning the digestion process. If you save any leftovers to feed at another time, it could cause the baby to become sick.

Paced feeding with acupressure

The other position would be to place baby upright. A baby

should always be held when being fed. It is NEVER appropriate to prop a bottle. Not only does this not provide the sense of comfort the baby craves and needs, it also is a choking hazard and can lead to respiratory aspiration. Baby should be held in an upright position with the bottle in a horizontal position. Tilt the bottle just slightly to fill the bottle nipple with milk. When the bottle is resting is a horizontal position in the baby's mouth rather than in a vertical position, the baby is forced to suck harder. This way the baby is working to get the milk out of the bottle, just as they work to get the milk out of the breast.

Halfway through feeding, remove the bottle, burp the baby, and switch sides. Just like with breastfeeding, baby will be expecting to switch sides to complete the feeding process. This provides good eye stimulation needed for development and prevents a "side preference" from developing. Burping halfway through the bottle allows less gas to be swallowed, resulting is less stomach upset. So, for example, if the bottle has 2 ounces of milk, feed 1 ounce and burp, then switch arms and feed the remainder of the bottle.

To burp, I recommend placing baby upright on your lap. Use the palm of your hand to apply ventral pressure on the baby's chest and use your thumb and middle finger to support the baby's cheeks. With the other hand, place your thumb and pinky under the baby's arm pits. Gently lift up and often the burp will come on out. If needed, you can apply firm pressure on the baby's back, rubbing up towards the shoulders.

Some prefer to pat the baby's back firmly. I personally am not a fan of that. Rubbing the air bubble out works far better, in my opinion.

If you have a stubborn air bubble, the alternate way (which will also calm a fussy baby) is to hold baby's knees together 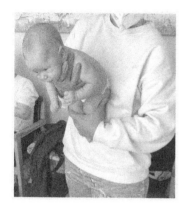 in one hand and push towards their chest. The other hand supports their chest and cheeks. Hold them in the center of your chest, get on your tippy toes, and bounce up and down. These are similar to toe lifts. The "bouncing" motion mimics what it was like when mom would walk with baby in utero. It again activates the "Du 2" acupressure point to centralize the nervous system.

An important note for heating breast milk. Never use a microwave, as the radiation will destroy the live properties of the milk, killing the antibodies. It also can cause hot patches within the bottle that can lead to burns within the mouth. I can't tell you how many times I have seen babies enter the ER with burns in their mouth and esophagus because of improper heating. Instead, heat the milk in a mug of hot water or in an electric bottle warmer. Prior to giving the bottle, make sure you test the temperature on your wrist. It should feel lukewarm.

Step 4: If baby is being really stubborn, try wrapping a shirt or nightgown that mom recently wore around the bottle. This will have momma's scent on it and may encourage the baby to feed. Face the baby out so she can see what is happening. Some babies get bored and need to see what is going on. You may need to incorporate movement as well such as rocking or bouncing.

Step 5: WHITE NOISE. This is one of the best inventions ever. I call it my magic wand. There are many white noise machines and apps out there. I usually recommend the Sound Sleeper app, which is free, on the vacuum cleaner setting. For those of you who are less tech savvy, you could turn on a good old-fashioned blow dryer or vacuum cleaner, or play static on the TV or radio. You can use anything really, but it must be loud and near the baby. They do of course sell portable white noise machines, which are okay, but they are typically not loud enough. You can have it loud; it will not hurt their ears. It will, however, make them stop crying like turning off a light switch. This will calm the baby neurologically, allowing them to eat more peacefully.

Step 6: Patience, patience, patience! This isn't going to be the smoothest transition, so the key is that you be patient and consistent. I promise you, your baby is not going to starve himself. Yes, he will protest, and he will probably go hours on end without feeding, but eventually the kid will eat. Babies are smart and stubborn, but they aren't self-destructive. Sooner or later, your little one will eat. It just takes time and patience.

Step 7. Consistency! I cannot stress this step enough. You have to be consistent. Try offering the bottle every hour, or every thirty minutes, for at least five minutes or so. If the baby screams and fights, stop, wait, and try again in thirty minutes. You don't want this to be a huge struggle. (I know, I know, it already is.) We want this to be a positive thing. If possible, first start introducing the bottle when baby is three to four weeks old, or whenever breastfeeding has been firmly established. Waiting to introduce a bottle after the eight week marker may cause a bigger issue, as baby is more aware of his surroundings. I recommend you bottle feed in place of one feeding, and be consistent with  which feeding that is. For example, every day the 5 p.m. feeding is a bottle. This way the baby gets in a routine, which babies need. Kids of all ages thrive on routine.

Right now it may seem overwhelming for you, but if you stick with it, your little one will eventually relax into her new routine.

The other part of being consistent is sticking to one bottle for a while. If you are changing out the bottle every attempt, it will confuse and frustrate both of you. Take it one day at a time.

There are babies that skip the bottle phase altogether. A breastfed baby can suck out of straw at three months of age, believe it or not. If you have delayed introducing a bottle till baby is older and more aware, usually around four months old, it will be more challenging. One thing you can try is offering freshly expressed breast milk in a sippy cup. Sit with your baby in front of mirror, grab yourself a cup with a straw, and show them how it is done. Babies want to be you, and they learn from watching you. If you make a game out of it, they will be more encouraged to try. There are many brands of sippy cups, and this too will be a process of trial and error. But I will say it is pretty awesome to skip the whole bottle process and go straight to the cup.

If your baby is STILL refusing the bottle or cup after all your attempts, find an IBCLC trained in oral ties to make sure there are no oral restrictions. Even if your baby has gained weight well, and has breastfed great, if there is a form of a tie in the mouth, the baby may gag and refuse the bottle, which may also mean she will refuse solids. The last thing you want is a feeding aversion. If that develops, the help of an OT (occupational therapist) will be needed.

I know that this can be so frustrating. Parenting is not for the weak. Hopefully this will give you a little bit more freedom to return to normalcy. Hang in there! It gets easier, and you are doing a wonderful job!

Chapter 17: Party Time with Eliminations

Just because you are breastfeeding does not mean that you can't let loose once in a while. You have spent months avoiding everything under the sun. No coffee, no alcohol, no unpasteurized cheese, no processed meats, no sushi, and obviously no smoking or recreational drugs. But do you still need to avoid all of that *after* baby is here? Absolutely not, with the exception of tobacco and recreational drugs, which should always be avoided. That should go without saying. Otherwise, it is all about moderation, my friend. If you want to have some brie and wine after your sushi dinner, with a latte the next morning, go for it. You deserve it! There are very few things that you have to pump and dump for. However, there are some moderations that do need to be kept in mind.

ALCOHOL

Let's start with alcohol since that seems to be the biggest concern. You can have a glass of wine or a beer, without concerns, just no keggers. Some women find that beer actually increases their supply because of the barley, hops, and brewer's yeast. However, the alcohol can inhibit oxytocin release and therefore should not be considered a galactagogue. Basically, the two things can cancel themselves out. Although alcohol does transfer into human milk readily, this does not mean that the dose of alcohol in the breastmilk is high. In actuality, the dose of alcohol transferred into milk is rather low, according to pharmacist Dr. Thomas Hale.[11]

According to a recent study, the maternal blood alcohol level must reach 300mg/dL before any side effects are reported in the baby. That is a lot of cocktails. So the rule of thumb is that if you are sober enough to drive, you are sober enough to breastfeed. If you have had a moderate amount of alcohol, avoid breastfeeding for at least two hours after drinking.

There is a new study that states that lactating mothers metabolize alcohol at a much faster rate. Dr. Hale states, "The state of lactation metabolically changes the rate of alcohol bioavailability. Blood alcohol levels were significantly lower in lactating women as compared to non-lactating women."[12]

Adult metabolism of alcohol is approximately one ounce in three hours. So a breastfeeding mom who drinks moderate amounts can basically feed once she feels neurologically normal. To make it easier to understand, one glass of wine you are good to go, but if you drink several drinks, you need to wait two hours after the last drink before you breastfeed. If you are completely hammered, do not breastfeed for at least eight hours. Drink tons of water and pump that milk out.

There are theories that, because alcohol does not freeze, you can pump out your "party milk," put it in the freezer, and in about three months' time the alcohol should rise to the top, leaving the frozen milk alcohol-free. This has been tested and shown to be true, but there are no published studies to back that up. Use common sense, and when in doubt, pump it out. If you are at a wedding and decide to have one drink, just be responsible.

The alcohol test strips that you can buy are not that accurate. I would not necessarily trust those over how you are feeling. If you feel hungover or tipsy, then obviously that round of margaritas hit you harder than you thought. You do not need an alcohol test strip to tell you whether or not you should time out pumping your milk. Trust your instincts.

MARIJUANA

I had to address this one, especially since there is so much conflicting information swirling around on the internet. Where I live in sunny SoCal, it is legal and encouraged for many chronic illnesses, as it is safer on the body than some of the harsher pharmaceuticals. However, does that make it safe for breastfeeding? According to the CDC and Dr. Hale, there is increasing concern about the use of cannabis products in breastfeeding mothers.

There have been multiple studies [13]showing that, depending on the method ingested, the amount of THC that is passed into the milk is low compared to the amount present in blood. Smoking pot seems to lead to more THC in breastmilk than ingesting marijuana, but due to the long-term effects observed in the infants even when small amounts are detected, it is strongly discouraged. Studies suggest that early infant exposure to cannabis may produce long-term changes in mental and motor developments. It is not worth it.

It also was discovered in a 2011 study [14]that THC is highly protein bound and is known to enter vascular areas such as the liver, heart, lung, and breast before accumulating in the fat tissue. This can allow for long-term exposure in the milk. There is a strong correlation between exposure to cannabis and decreased prolactin levels. So not only will it pass into the milk with a risk of sedation for your baby, it has the potential to significantly impact your pituitary response to prolactin, thus lowering your supply. The forty-five minutes of being "high" is not worth the risk it poses to the baby or to your supply.

NICOTINE

I would hope that it would go without saying that smoking cigarettes, E-CIGs, or vapes, is a big no for pregnancy and breastfeeding. However, as someone who used to smoke occasionally in college, I understand that can be a battle. The first thing I am going to recommend is to quit, which can be hard. Nicotine patches, gum, and pretty much any medication to help you quit does have some nicotine in it but is far safer for breastfeeding than continuing to smoke. So I am turning to my good pal Dr. Hale for the scientific effect that nicotine has on breastmilk and the baby.

In a recent study[15], researchers compared women who had around seventeen cigarettes a day with those who used a nicotine patch. They concluded that nicotine does in fact transfer into breastmilk via a 21mg patch at the same rate and amount as a mother who smoked close to seventeen cigarettes a day. What also may surprise you is that the amount of nicotine transferred into the breast milk is more than double what is passed through the placenta in pregnancy. However, using a 14mg or 7mg patch decreased the nicotine intake by the infant up to 70% and had no significant influence on the milk intake of the infant. The lower-dose patch is therefore a safer option than continued smoking—duh—but interestingly enough, it also better than nicotine gum. Maternal blood levels of nicotine gum averaged 30–60% of those found in smokers. So while transdermal patches produce a sustained and lower plasma level, the gum produced large variations, especially when chewed rapidly, mimicking similar fluctuations for inhalation.

That was a lot of science I threw out there. To sum up, just do not smoke. It isn't good for you or your baby. If you are a smoker and are having a difficult time quitting, use a nicotine patch rather than gum, as that is safer for the baby. There are medications such as Wellbutrin that do help some people stop smoking quickly, but you should consult with your doctor about your particular case. You probably don't ever want your kids becoming smokers, so don't start them out early with your milk.

CAFFEINE

Girl….I know you are tired, so let's talk coffee, lattes, espresso, even a Coke (the carbonated kind, obviously; street drugs are a big no-no). I tell moms that drinking coffee is fine as long as it is done in moderation. A cup of Joe early in the morning is fine, but don't drink four shots of espresso. Caffeine is a central nervous system stimulant that is present in many foods and drinks, including chocolate. (You can eat chocolate, by the way; it isn't going to cause your baby to be gassy or have reflux. Go eat some Dove chocolate on me.)

The half-life of caffeine in an adult is around four to six hours (half-life is a measure of how long it stays in your system; it measures how long it takes for half of the substance to leave your body). For newborns, it is over ninety-seven hours. Good news is that the half-life decreases as the baby gets older. By three months it drops to fourteen hours, and by six months, it is two and a half hours. Peak levels of caffeine are found in breastmilk 60–120 minutes after ingestion. There is some evidence to support that chronic coffee drinking can lower the iron content of your milk. Drinking coffee also can dehydrate you, which is why it is important to up your water intake. You should already be drinking half your body weight in ounces of water, but if you drink a caffeinated drink, you need to counter it with eight ounces of water.

Occasional use of caffeine is fine. If you want to drink coffee every day, just know that there will be high plasma levels in your baby, particularly in the first twelve weeks. Symptoms of too much caffeine in your baby would be agitation, irritability, rapid heart rate, poor sleeping pattern… basically the same effect it would have on you. Personally, as tired as I was as a new mom, having one cup of coffee in the morning made me a better mom and less of a zombie. I am sure many of you will feel the same. In my opinion, as long as you understand the side effects it can have, go make a Starbucks run, girl. You have earned it!

DAIRY/SOY

Since we are on the topic of elimination of things in your diet, I wanted to briefly touch on the crazy elimination diets that pediatricians place on mothers in hopes of decreasing gas, fussiness, green poop, etc.

By this point of the book, we have learned that colic isn't really a thing. Gas and reflux are usually caused by oral ties and poor latch technique, and green poop is not automatically due to dairy sensitivity. Yet the minute the baby starts to be fussy, the first thing the pediatrician will tell you to do is cut out dairy and soy. You can spot a dairy-sensitive baby a mile away. The hair sticks straight up as if they licked a light socket, they have horrible eczema, and their poop is green and mucousy with streaks of blood in it. This is my gorgeous daughter Alaina when she was about six months old. She is the perfect example of a dairy-sensitive baby. Eczema on her face, hair sticking up, and she had smelly green poops with streaks of blood. Her pediatrician of course told me to stop giving her breast milk and to switch to a hypoallergenic formula that was still diary based, was expensive as hell, and smelled like rusty

My daughter Alaina age 6 mo

aluminum. So gross all around. It never made sense to me why I would swap out my breastmilk for a formula that was based off of a bovine protein. Nevertheless, if this is truly an issue it is far easier (though not easy) to eliminate dairy and soy from your diet than to give formula, unless you as a mom cannot do elimination diets.

Dairy and soy are best friends and work similarly in the gut. It isn't a lactose intolerance—we need lactose to digest any form of milk—it is a bovine protein issue. Soy reacts the same way. These proteins are harder to digest and can ferment in the gut. You do not need to be a label reader, you just need to eliminate the big items: milk, yogurt, cream, tofu, edamame, etc.

If your baby is fussy but has normal-looking poop (yellow and seedy), perfect skin, and gorgeous hair, chances are the fussiness has nothing to do with what you are eating, and everything to do with how your baby is eating.

I have seen moms come into my office frustrated and starving because their pediatrician has asked them to go on a strict elimination diet of no eggs, dairy, soy, nuts, some fruits, and the list goes on. Basically, they can have lettuce. For one, that is annoying as hell, and second, where are you going to get the calories and protein you need to make milk? It is a lose-lose battle.

If you are being told you need to cut anything out of your diet, my recommendation would be first to consult with an IBCLC to rule out any other possible cause of the gas, have the baby's poop tested for blood, and take a look at your baby's physicality. Spiky hair means dairy care! There is no reason to stress yourself out, which will only cause more issues down the road, if the baby's temperament has absolutely nothing to do with you.

Chapter 18: What If I Get Sick or Catch the RONA!

It is inevitable, Momma, you will get sick sooner or later with something. Kids are walking, adorable petri dishes who touch EVERYTHING and decide that all objects large or small belong in their mouths, noses, and ears. Once your little critter begins having playdates or, worse, enters the cesspool that is daycare, the sticky germs will inhabit your home.

Babies are born with very fragile immune systems. They technically get their first natural "inoculation" when they pass through the birth canal. If you happened to poop while pushing, as gross as that sounds, it does help give your baby their first exposure to your germs and begins the foundation of their immune system. God knew what He was doing when he placed the vagina near the sewer hole and required the same muscles to poop and bring life into this world. I am constantly amazed at the intricate design and details of our bodies. If you had a cesarean birth, do not fret, your sweet one encounters germs that way also, just a different route.

This is why, above all else, providing colostrum is so crucial because it is meant to close the gut and begin the process of building immunity. It is rich in antibodies and is *the* most important thing your fresh newborn can receive. If you are only able to provide colostrum to your baby and nothing else, consider yourself proud. You did not fail. You are a magnificent superhero who gave your baby the best start possible in life.

I mentioned in the first few chapters of this book how the baby's saliva absorbs into your breast and your immune system reacts to provide antibodies for your baby should the little one be sick. Yet what happens if you get sick first? Or worse, what if you catch Covid? Do you quarantine or isolate with your baby? Or do you pass the baby off to your partner and hope for the best? What if you have a stomach flu or food poisoning? Is it smart to keep breastfeeding or will that dehydrate you and risk passing the bacteria onto the baby? These are the many questions that swirl around in our heads at the wee hours of the night, because as soon as we birth a baby, not only are we transformed into mothers, we are also magically transformed into the biggest worrywarts that ever existed.

BREATHE...as best as you can, that is. The single most important thing you can do as a mother in this moment is to continue to breastfeed. I know you feel wretched and a fussy baby on you is probably the last thing you want, but it will transform how your baby recovers in this moment. Your body will create magical antibodies against whatever virus or bacteria you are fighting and will transfer them through your breastmilk to your baby. This is why so often, out of everyone in the household, the baby is the only one who does not get sick. You have basically created an antidote for them.

Right now, you now need to continue to take care of yourself so that you can also support your milk supply. If you do not focus on getting well, your baby cannot continue to stay well. Now, there is always the chance that the baby will get sick also. If this happens, do not panic. Look at it as a mini blessing that is building and strengthening that fragile immune system. The more that immune system is exposed to germs, the more protective it can become. Breastmilk then handles everything else.

Step 1: Stay as hydrated as you possibly can. Keep your electrolytes up. If you are fighting a stomach bug and are struggling to keep anything down, take small sips of Gatorade or Body Armour to keep as much fluid in as you can. It is absolutely safe to take antiemetic medications (the no-more-barfing meds) and anti-diarrhea medications. That is safe to pass on to the baby. I personally am terrified of vomiting and am proud to say I have been vomit-free since '93! So I will do anything in my power to stop that. Most people are not like me and know they will feel better if they just puke it out. Whatever your philosophy is, roll with it. Here is a mom hack for you: Benadryl is an amazing antiemetic. It stops nausea and barfing. Every household should have this. Now, typically I give caution moms about taking Benadryl, as this is an antihistamine that can lower supply for some mothers.

But in this instance, the priority it to keep fluids in you. Do what you can.

Step 2: If you have a fever, allow it to continue for a while, as the purpose of the fever is to fight off whatever is making you ill. However, fevers can dehydrate you faster than anything. You can take Tylenol (acetaminophen) or Motrin or Advil (ibuprofen) to break your fever if needed and treat body aches. This will not affect your milk supply in any way and is perfectly safe to pass onto the baby. Remember, most medications you take are safe for baby while breastfeeding, as your liver breaks them down first. If you are concerned about a medication, you can reach out to your pharmacist, IBCLC, or pediatrician, and they should be able to guide you. If not, reach out to me. If you would rather a more holistic or homeopathic route, belladonna pellets are a wonderful way to break a fever and fast. Place five pellets under your tongue every hour until your fever breaks. You can also do the water trick that I mentioned in the mastitis section.

Step 3: If you are congested or coughing or have other symptoms of a respiratory infection, this gets a bit trickier. Medications to treat this are safe to pass through your milk to your baby, but they will lower your supply drastically. Your breasts are mucus membranes, just like your nose is. The decongestant will dry up your milk supply in the same way it dries up your congestion. You also need to stay away from anything with menthol, eucalyptus, or peppermint, as that will also affect supply. Here is a list of things to avoid if possible while sick, as they will lower your supply:

- Sudafed or any OTC medication that decongests
- Vicks or any form of menthol ointments
- Cough drops that contain menthol or eucalyptus
- Afrin nose spray
- Peppermint essential oils, Breathe from DoTerra
- Cloves, oregano (which is a natural antibiotic)

Anything containing any form of a decongestant is a big no-no, but that does not mean that there is nothing you can do to help your symptoms. For congestion, I would recommend sinus rinses, like NeilMed or Netti Pot. Make sure you remember to include the saline packets. I once forgot to put the saline into the water before a sinus rinse….OWIE! Literally one of the worst pains of my life, and I have been through some doozies. Saline is a natural sterilizer, and it helps to push out any virus or bacteria along with the snot. It is super gross and satisfying at the same time.

You can also use nose strips to open up the sinus cavity. There also are many types of homeopathic remedies that are safe for breastfeeding such as Boiron Coldcalm and Hyland's Kids Cold and Cough. Large amounts of vitamin C are also encouraged.

Step 4: Rest. (Cue laugh and eye roll from every tired mother out there). This is probably the hardest thing to do. When you're a mom, there is no such thing as rest, to be quite honest, especially if you and your child are sick together. Just when you finally fall asleep, a kid is going to puke all over you or start crying from earaches. I think this is one of the many examples of how moms are badass compared to anyone else. We do not let a little sniffle stop us from being a superpower healer. All jokes aside, if you can, sleep when your baby sleeps. Call in help from family and friends so you can try and get well. If you do not find a way to get better, the whole family dynamic can crumble. I am the absolute worst with this. To me, rest is a terrible four letter word, but it is a lesson I have had to learn to pay attention to. If you do not provide self-care, you will end up far worse than when you started.

In recent years (depending on when you are reading this), the Covid pandemic has affected every aspect of life, especially parenting. Covid-19 is not like any of the other coronaviruses we have encountered in the past. It has a mind of its own and has changed the game of healthcare.

As if parenting wasn't hard enough, now we had to throw a deadly pandemic into the mix. Regardless of where you stand on mask and vaccines, one thing that is true is that breastmilk has been proven to help fight Covid-19. A recent study published in *JAMA Pediatrics*, co-authored by scientists at the University of Rochester Medical Center and New York University, found substantial evidence that breastfeeding mothers who have either received the mRNA vaccine or contracted COVID and recovered produced SARS-coV-2 antibodies in their breast milk.[16] Mothers who had acquired vaccine immunity produced powerful immunoglobulin G (IgG) antibodies and those women who had disease-acquired immunity produced potent levels of immunoglobulin A (IgA).

Scientists took samples of breastmilk from each group of participating mothers, one containing the vaccinated antibodies and the other containing disease-acquired antibodies, and infected the samples with live SARS-CoV-2. Both types of antibodies neutralized the virus, meaning it basically killed the virus. Is anyone else wondering why in the world we are not using breastmilk to end this thing? As if we didn't already have enough reasons to normalize breastfeeding, let's add killing Covid-19 to the mix!

An assistant professor in the Division of Pediatric Allergy and Immunology at URMC stated, "It's one thing to measure antibody concentrations, but it's another to say that antibodies are functional and can neutralize the SARS-CoV-2 virus." The beautiful piece of this is that it didn't matter which route was used to achieve antibodies. Both worked to nullify Covid. Can I get a hallelujah!

So what does this mean for breastfeeding moms who are currently sick with the virus? It means keep breastfeeding! Your super milk is saving your baby's immune system. In fact, I would recommend giving everyone in your family a dose of your milk. I know it may seem a bit weird for some, but if you are capable of making the antidote to Covid, I would strongly recommend sharing the love, girl. The above picture is of pumped milk over the course of a few days. The bag on the left is pumped on a day prior to becoming infected with Covid. The bag on the right is several days into the virus. You can see

the immediate change in the mother's milk. What is most interesting is that, usually when a mother is sick and pumps, the milk has a yellow tint to it from the leukocytes and various antibodies present. When the pumping mother has Covid, her milk turns green. This shows the visible process of her body fighting the virus and passing those live antibodies into the baby, essentially providing a small version of the vaccine. It also shows just how different of a beast this thing is.

By now we all know that this virus is smart and likes to constantly mutate. It does not discriminate based on age, race, or gender. No one is safe, and now with Omicron, children are more affected that ever. Many patients of mine, including babies as young as six weeks, have ended up in the NICU with Covid pneumonia. It is a force to be reckoned with, but each day we are becoming stronger, and I truly believe that we can end this pandemic one lactating breast at a time. If you happen to get sick, follow the same advice as you would for any other illness. Wear a mask around your baby and take care of yourself. And most importantly, breastfeed as often as you can.

Chapter 19: What No One Tells You About

If you haven't figured out by now, there are a ton of books, classes, seminars, and YouTube videos to prepare you for pregnancy, birth, parenting, and breastfeeding (and now more, thanks to this new gem of a book), but there is a whole side to breastfeeding that no one really talks about. Well, girl, get ready because I am about to spill the tea on all the hidden secrets. I want you to be fully prepared for what is about to come. I always hated this secret "hazing/initiation" into motherhood because no one was willing to talk about the embarrassing moments. I've got you. Here we go.

In the sex chapter, we talked about how when you have an orgasm, your milk lets down and you spray everywhere, all while you have sandpaper for a vagina because all your bodily fluids disperse to other parts of the body. Yep, that one was a shocker for me. In another chapter, we talked about how quickly your breasts, nipples, and areolas can change in size and color. Some women have nipples the size of pencil erasers, while others have nipples that grow to the size of a quarter. No one is EVER prepared for that one. You have heard that there are drastic changes, but seeing it is completely different. We have even discussed that, even though you began leaking colostrum at twenty-four weeks of pregnancy, creating yellow crusty nipples, your mature milk may take up to five to ten days post-delivery to fully come in, which is incredibly confusing but completely normal!

When it came to writing this chapter, I wanted to get other mothers' points of view, so I went to Instagram and asked women to tell me the one thing that no one told them about breastfeeding that caught them off guard. Despite the overwhelming feeling of being underprepared, the first and most common answer was how shocked women were with how painful breastfeeding could be, and more importantly that this pain although common is an indication of a problem. Not just nipple pain, but engorgement pain, clogged duct pain, pump pain, all of it. You are told to expect it to hurt for a bit and then transition to rainbows and roses, not toe-curling pain. They all were surprised to find out that pain is not normal, and means something needs to be adjusted. Here are some of their responses:

1. The fact that it hurts way more than labor and birth ever did.
2. The cramping of your uterus immediately after your baby latches in postpartum. I thought my contractions were over. Didn't know that breastfeeding would cause that strong of a response the first few hours after birth.
3. Electric nipples! The pain when your milk lets down feels like an electric shock.

4. It is HARD! F%@king hard! Hands down the most difficult thing I have ever had to do.

5. How badly you want it to work, and how guilty you feel when it doesn't work.

6. That you would be caught in a constant information tug-of-war with your pediatrician, specifically about ties.

7. Everyone tells you something different. The hospital LC will contradict the private practice IBCLC. The nurse tells you the opposite of what every lactation specialist tells you. Your OB says one thing while the pediatrician says the complete opposite, leaving you with no clue who to believe.

8. Google is not always right—in fact, it is usually wrong—yet I still am so addicted to it and am convinced I am a doctor now!

9. Baby brain does not go away right away (TRUTH! I still have baby brain twenty years later)

10. So much of breastfeeding is about mental toughness and positive mindset.

11. That you will get an overwhelming feeling of exhaustion when you breastfeed. Tryptophan overload every single time, to the point where you can barely keep your eyes open.

12. How constantly hungry you are, yet you never feel satisfied and you are always worrying if what you eat is going to affect your breastmilk or give baby gas.

13. How thirsty you get, no matter how much you drink. I never felt more like a camel in my life.
14. How much your birth can affect your breastfeeding outcome. So different with each baby.
15. You will probably feed every time the baby wakes up, not just every three to four hours. If you are not ready to wake up every few hours for months on end, do not have a baby.
16. The length of a feed or the minutes do not matter after a few weeks. Baby can be done eating in three minutes and will have taken almost 3 oz. Every baby is different.
17. It can make you incredibly happy yet sad at the same time. All I heard was negative things, was not expecting the bonding to be so intense.
18. The mental gymnastics involved!
19. Cluster feeds mean growth spurt; it does not mean low supply.
20. That your milk comes out like a showerhead. There are eight to ten nipple pores. I was expecting it to be like a squirt gun.
21. How often you leak and need to change your breast pads.
22. The other boob leaks while the baby is nursing from the other one.
23. Night shirts and night bras are not cute but definitely worth the money.

24. Wearing an underwire bra may cause you to get clogged ducts.
25. Sleeping on your stomach feels like sleeping on two hard watermelons.
26. The breast will never be fully empty, it just starts right back up again. You will always be able to express something.
27. Support from your partner can make or break breastfeeding.
28. That at four months, feedings change drastically. They become distracted, turn their heads to look around, taking your nipple with them.
29. Once they start solids at six months, they only need twenty-four ounces of breastmilk or formula a day if they are eating three times a day.
30. How confusing all the pump parts are, and how hard it is to decide what supplies to buy.
31. Some women gain weight, not lose weight.
32. High palates and clicking are a sign of a tongue tie.
33. Lip blisters are a warning sign of a bigger problem, and are not "normal" like the doctor said.
34. That you can experience a letdown from hearing a baby cry on TV or even from a cat meowing.
35. You have to measure your nipples for your pump flange to get adequate milk removal, and one nipple may be a completely different size than the other one.

36. That your baby can get bored while feeding and start scratching, biting, or pinching the other nipple with their hand.
37. That you can have multiple letdowns.
38. Sleeping through the night for a baby is six hours, so plan accordingly.
39. Your relaxin hormone doesn't go away right away and you can have carpel tunnel.
40. Breastmilk changes flavor and that can make your baby's breath smell weird.
41. Mom guilt is brutal. That as hard as all this was, one day you will miss it terribly.

I can relate with every single one of these statements. Every…single…one. Momma, I wasn't kidding when I said it takes a village. This is why I have a job. As I was reading the list, a few more things came to mind that I wanted to add or elaborate on.

NURSING STRIKES

Another frustrating thing for mothers are nursing strikes. These are a common occurrence and most of the time they are short lived. Sometimes, this is your baby's way of letting you know you are missed. Very sweet…adorable maybe, but frustrating nonetheless. There are other reasons, however, that a baby would go on a nursing strike. Things to look for if the strike lasts longer than twenty-four hours:

a) If the baby is around the three-month mark, chances are it is a hormone flux and the flavor and flow of your milk are different, which of course means ovulation. Oh joy! This is where the magnesium trick I mentioned earlier comes into play.

b) Is the baby pulling at his ears or crying when being laid down? It is possible that there is an ear infection or fluid in the eustachian tubes. Check for fever, congestion, watery eyes, and snotty nose. Ear infections can come on fast, so even if the baby is good in the morning, by evening it could be a raging infection.

c) Between three to six months, the teething process begins. Check to see if the baby has any swollen gums or is constantly trying to put hands and objects into her mouth. Granted, that is part of how they discover themselves and their environment, but if there is drool city happening, and baby is biting, chances are there is a tooth about to erupt.

d) What is the urine like? Sometimes when a baby has a UTI (urinary tract infection), it affects how they will eat. This one often gets overlooked. If the urine is dark in color, has a strong odor, and baby is crying more frequently, it may be worth exploring.

e) Thrush may also be happening. We talked about this earlier in the book. For the baby, it will look like white fur all over the mouth, on the tongue, cheeks, and inside of the lips. It is very painful. Your kiddo however will probably be resisting all forms of eating if this is the case. This will need to be treated with anti-fungal treatments.

SIBLINGS

Second-time moms will feel as if they do not need to prepare as much because they have been through this before. Yet having more than one baby, especially if your kids are close in age, can bring its own set of surprises. Do not be surprised if your toddler asks to breastfeed, even if it has been months or years since that child was last on the breast. Most likely it is more about feeling left out than it is about actually wanting to breastfeed.

My girls are twenty-one months a part. I weaned Alyssa at nine months. It did not even cross my mind that she would be even slightly interested in breastfeeding. The sibling rivalry began early. She basically wanted what she couldn't have. I feel like this is the basis of most things in life. I kept telling her no, momma's milk was for the baby. She kept pushing, and I finally gave in and allowed her to try it. As soon as it wasn't something of mystery to her any longer, she couldn't have cared less. Again, this was just her trying to understand her role in all of this, as this new pumpkin came into her life like a wrecking ball.

The best piece of advice that was given to me when I had my second baby was to create a sibling nursing basket. Basically it was a laundry basket I filled up with toys, books, and coloring things that she could only have when I was breastfeeding. She became my biggest cheerleader. I would put the basket up high so she couldn't reach it and would set the timer at the end of each feed so she knew when she would have the chance to play with the toys again. This was a lifesaver. Instead of breastfeeding being something that took her mommy away from her, it became a game that she was able to play along with me. I also included a doll so she could have a baby to care for when I had to care for my baby. It worked like a charm and made her feel like the Super Sibling that she was. (Yes, there was a superhero cape in there as well. She is still as infatuated with superheroes now as she was then. I blame Marvel.) It gave me the chance to focus on breastfeeding her sister.

Of course, when baby sister began to crawl and tried to take the toys in said basket, that basket was then turned over and placed on top of her sister like a mini cage. I walked around the corner as I heard screaming to find Alyssa sitting on the laundry basket, placed on top of her sister. Ahhhh, the sisterly bond began so early.

TANDEM FEEDING

This is basically when you feed two of your little ones at once. Typically it is used for feeding twins but can also refer to when you begin feeding a new baby while continuing to feed your toddler. You can absolutely feed both babies at the same time, but that does require some practice and loads of patience. The older child basically can function as your pump.

When the new baby arrives, I do recommend feeding the newborn first so that the nutrients and amount of milk your body makes can be determined by the infant. After feeding the newborn, the toddler can always have a turn. The older child will have a stronger suck and is able to take the place of your pump. After all, your kid will be a far cuter pump than the electric one.

It is safe to breastfeed your older child while pregnant with your new baby if your OB/GYN feels that it is safe to do so. If you are at risk for preterm delivery, then it would be wise to avoid any form of nipple stimulation. Your supply will most likely dip when you are pregnant because of the change in hormones. You cannot take most galactagogues while pregnant, so it is important to decide, depending on the age of your nursling, if supplementation is needed. After the delivery, I would try to give as much of your colostrum to the new baby as possible. If the sibling has some, that is awesome, but with the fragility of the new baby's immune system, it would be highly beneficial to his/her gut.

If you are giving birth to twins, I highly recommend having an IBCLC work with you so that you can create a schedule that is not overwhelming and learn how to help your supply. God gave you two breasts for a reason. You truly only need one breast to fully feed a baby. The second one is the bonus boob. Breastfeeding twins can seem overwhelming, but it is absolutely doable. The key is finding a schedule that will work for all of you.

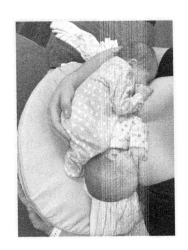

WHAT NOT TO SAY TO THE BREASTFEEDING MOTHER

When you become a mother, and especially if you choose to breastfeed, everyone you know will have pearls of wisdom for you. They'll offer advice on how to feed the baby, dress the baby, and care for the baby. However, this is YOUR baby, and you get to do this YOUR way! So take everything with a grain of salt.

Even women who haven't breastfed their own children, or maybe don't know a lot about the art of breastfeeding, will give unsolicited advice to nursing mothers. They mean well, but they sometimes give advice that isn't exactly helpful. In fact, it is downright hurtful, but you may be way too exhausted to correct them. So if anyone is giving unsolicited advice, send this section there way. Without further ado… here is what you do not say to a breastfeeding mother and what you DO say in return:

"Are you sure you have enough milk? That baby wants to eat all the time!"

Remember, the breasts work by supply and demand. The more they are stimulated, the more milk a woman will produce. The quickest way to make a mother doubt her natural ability to make milk is by questioning whether or not her breasts are even capable of doing the job. Of course the baby wants to eat all the time—that is what healthy normal newborns do! They eat eight to twelve times in a twenty-four-hour period and even more when there is a growth spurt.

"Your milk looks really thin…are you sure there is enough fat and calories in that?"

Breastmilk is supposed to look thin, but that doesn't mean it does not have the caloric properties needed to feed a baby adequately. Formula has a different protein than human milk, one that actually sits and churns in the baby's stomach, which is why formula can sometimes cause more gas and stomach upset. Formula is going to look different because it is different.

308

"I thought breastfeeding was supposed to make you lose your baby weight?"

Are you kidding me? Why would anyone say this to a new mother? Getting back to your pre-baby body takes time. Your uterus needs time to shrink back to its original pear shape and size (two to four inches). It took nine months to get you to your current state, and for some women it takes nine months to get back. Breastfeeding does burn a lot of calories, 1500 a day extra, to be exact. So it is true that women who breastfeed will get back to their pre-pregnant size before non-breastfeeding women. However, it still will not be an overnight process. Be patient, give your body a chance to recoup!

"Add cereal to the baby's bottle. It will make them sleep longer!"

The American Academy of Pediatrics now advises parents to wait to introduce solid foods until the infant is six months old. This is because the baby's digestive system is not mature enough to digest and handle solid foods until this time. Cereal and other solids replaces breast milk with a less ideal food, and the last thing you want to do is to replace the baby's main source of nutrition. Numerous studies have shown that giving cereal to an infant does NOT help babies sleep through the night, nor does it help with reflux. Honestly, cereal should be avoided all together, as there isn't much value nutritionally. At least wait until advised by the child's pediatrician.

"Are you really going to breastfeed in here?!"

Yes...yes, she is! Where a woman chooses to breastfeed her baby is completely and entirely up to her! This is her baby and her breasts. If it makes you uncomfortable, then you may need to go elsewhere rather than making the mother feel ashamed for doing what her breasts were intended to do—feed a baby. This is a personal choice that should be decided by the mother only, and it should be respected. Breastfeeding is just as normal as you eating a sandwich, and every human, regardless of age, should be allowed to feel comfortable eating anywhere they so choose.

The most important thing for family members and friends to remember is that this new mother is giving her baby the best food possible. The best thing anyone can do is to support the new mother's decision to breastfeed, even if there are personal doubts about breastfeeding from an outsider. Support is the key for both the new mother and her partner. Don't attribute every baby problem to breastfeeding. Remember, the new family is learning. By supporting a breastfeeding mom each step of the way, you will help make those first days with the new baby easier for everyone, and she will feel more confident as the days go on.

Chapter 20: Biting and Solids

You are nursing your seven-month-old baby when, out of nowhere, he clamps down, biting your nipple. You impulsively let out a high-pitched shriek due to the sharp pain, which of course startles the baby, and both of you look suddenly dazed and confused. What in the world caused that, you may ask? Your baby now has teeth, and with that teething process comes biting on everything—including you! So what does this mean for your breastfeeding relationship? A lot of moms think this means they have to wean, even if they don't want to. This could not be further from the truth! Biting should not be a reason to quit breastfeeding. This is a temporary problem with an easy fix.

If your baby is nursing correctly, you should not feel her teeth, even if there is a whole mouth full. The tongue covers the teeth while nursing, so it is physically impossible for a baby to nurse and bite at the same time. Babies bite for several reasons, and it often varies based on their age.

As we now know, a newborn may bite or clamp down (long before having teeth) simply due to a position change. If a baby is at all on her back while nursing, with mother leaning towards the baby, the infant will feel a sense of alarm and will bite down out of fear of losing the food source. If the nursing mother has a fast letdown, the baby may bite in order to control the flow of milk, similar to clamping down a hose to slow down the gush.

Biting is a behavior that most babies will try, especially while teething. I will never forget the first time Alyssa bit me. Baby teeth are like tiny razors. One night, I was feeding her in the middle of the night. I was half asleep and she clearly was not. Out of the blue, she clamped down and I literally saw stars. I screamed, which startled her, and she immediately started crying. I felt so bad for scaring her, but she never did it again.

Usually, biting is a temporary issue that only lasts for a few days to a couple of weeks. But rest assured that if your little one is a nibbler, this learned behavior can be stopped with a little persistence from the mother. Each baby is different, and it may take various strategies to find a solution. What works will most likely depend on the baby's age, temperament, and personality. Babies are people pleasers, and they want their mom to be happy. Most of the time, your little critter has no clue that what he is doing hurts you. His gums hurt, or he is bored, so chewing on the one thing that gives them comfort seems like the perfect solution. If your sweet one decides to chomp down, here are a few steps to help you through:

1. PRIOR TO FEEDING: If the baby is known to bite at the beginning of a nursing session, it may be due to tension in the jaw or sore teething gums. Teething is

the most common reason that babies begin to bite down. Try some gum massage. Stick a clean index finger inside the baby's mouth, and gently massage the lower gumline. Encourage the baby to bite down on your finger to release that tension. Be sure to stay along the gumline so you don't gag the child. If teeth have erupted, you may want to use a cool teething toy instead of your finger, as these little ones, as cute as they are, have been known to cause some fierce marks. Better the toy or your finger then your nipple though! Practice good latching techniques and make sure that the baby is latched deeply. Give positive reinforcement when the baby latches correctly! Even at this young of age, babies will respond well to high praise.

2.   BITING AT THE END OF A FEED: The majority of the time, biting happens toward the end of a feed when the baby is getting bored or is no longer hungry. This behavior is most common in older babies rather than newborns. If you notice a pattern of biting towards the end, watch for cues that your baby is bored and end the nursing session before they have a chance to bite. You should be able to tell right before the baby bites based on rising tension in his jaw. Simply remove him from the breast and end the nursing session. If the baby is biting out of boredom, he will happily move on

to another activity.

3. A DISTRACTED BABY: If your baby seems easily distracted (which is very common as babies get older, specifically around four months of age), don't force a feeding session. It will end up backfiring on you and give her more excuses to bite you. Around this age, a baby's eyesight matures and he is able to see color for the first time. Imagine if you had only seen in black and white your whole life, and then boom your world turned into the "Wizard Of Oz." Everything is new and exciting. Of course you are going to get distracted while eating. Dad or big sister walks in, and your baby turns to look at the new face, taking your nipple with them. If only they knew that your breasts were not made of Play-Doh, although at the end of breastfeeding they may feel like it. (Insert saggy boob joke here.)

Your kiddo will happily pull your nipple every which way as he checks out the new surroundings. He may even reach over and begin playing with your other nipple, which is a survival instinct to increase the flow of milk with extra nipple stimulation. If he is wiggling, pushing against you, or pops on and off several times in a row, he may be having difficulty staying focused on the task at hand or trying to send a message to you that the breast is empty or the flow of milk is changing and frustrating him. Try going into a dark, quiet room, eliminating as many sensory distractions as possible. Lay down with your baby and attempt again. If the baby is still seeming distracted, it very well may be he isn't hungry or simply needs guidance in keeping him focused. One thing I have found that helps tremendously is a nursing necklace. These are colorful beads that you can wear around your neck that the baby can grasp onto. Or hook a dangling toy to your bra strap to help entertain him.

4. BITING FOR YOUR ATTENTION: Some babies choose to bite as a way of getting attention. If you notice that the biting seems to happen when you are talking on the phone, or simply talking in general, it may be that your baby is requiring a little extra alone time with his momma! Put down all distractions and look at your little one. Welcome the quiet distraction to your busy day. This will also allow you a chance to be able to watch for those "biting cues."

So what to do if the biting continues? Th simplest and most effective way is to end the nursing session. This will teach the baby that nursing and biting do NOT go together. Calmly remove the baby and gently tell him, "No, thank you!" It is not a good idea to scream at the baby as a means to get him to stop, although it is totally understandable if the baby catches you by surprise! Yelling on purpose, however, may have the opposite effect of what you want. Either the baby will think it is funny and continue to bite for a reaction, or he will be frightened and then decide to go on a nursing strike. Neither option is fun. Ending the nursing session will send the message and eventually end the behavior.

Positive reinforcement, of course, goes a long way with nursing babies, even the newborns. Praise your baby when he latches correctly. In the meantime, if your nipples are super sore, or if the skin has been broken, I recommend using some gel pads until the abrasions have healed. If you have to use a nipple shield or give that breast a break, that is absolutely fine. The good news is this is temporary, and with a little perseverance and a sprinkle of patience, you can continue to have a positive breastfeeding experience for however long you and you baby desire.

Since we are on the topic of teeth and biting, I felt it was important to talk about the introduction of solid foods. That first year of life, breastmilk or formula is the baby's primary source of food. Solids are simply complementary. There are some added nutrients, but the primary point is to get their body and them used to eating.

The following is a month-by-month feeding schedule to be used as a guide for your infant's growth. Every baby is different and will have unique growth patterns, but this chart can be used as a guide to ensure that your baby is getting the proper amount of nutrition for her age.

It is always recommended that you slowly introduce new foods into a child's diet, especially those that could be a potential allergen. This way if an allergy is present, it will be easier to determine which food was the culprit. The most important factor, however, is your baby's feeding cues. Your baby will be the one to tell you when he is having a growth spurt, when he is ready for solids, and which type of food he prefers. Your job as the parent is to be aware of these cues, feed them appropriately, and guide them into a future of good feeding habits.

The following chart shows types of foods and amounts appropriate for most babies according to each specific age group. For the first six months, the amount of breastmilk needed for infant growth is estimated at two and half to three times their body weight in ounces per day. For example, your eight pound baby would require (after the first week of life) between 20 and 24 ounces a day. As they grow, the number of ounces needed also grows, until they begin eating different types of food. Then it will return to a 24-ounce minimum.

When introducing solids such as vegetables and fruits, it is a good idea to start with the vegetables so your baby will be more willing eat them. Fruit, as we know, is much sweeter than our veggies, so babies who have fruit before veggies aren't as interested. Who would want to eat mushed peas when you can have juicy peaches? Studies have shown that when veggies are introduced prior to fruit, babies adjust to a more well-rounded diet.

All babies will differ in appetite and readiness for solid food. Over the years, there have been changes in the advice given about when to introduce other foods. Currently, the AAP recommends six months of age, or when the baby shows interest, is able to sit up, and the tongue thrust reflex is gone.

Many philosophies exist such as "baby-led weaning" or preparing your own food versus buying jars of baby food. Truly it is a personal choice and one I would talk to your pediatrician about in depth. They may be able to guide you on the specifics of what your baby needs.

AGE	APPROPRIATE FOODS	AMOUNT
0-2 months (0-8weeks)	Breastmilk or Newborn formula **Can't overfeed a breastfed infant. You can overfeed a FORMULA fed infant. Newborn formula	Feed on demand 8 or more x in 24 hour period (Baby should regain birth weight between 10-14 days of life. Normal infant weight gain is 4-7 oz a week) 2-3 oz every 3 hours. (based on infants weight baby should receive between 16-28oz a day)
2-4 months	Breastmilk iron fortified formula	Feed on demand 6 or more times in 24 hours 4-6 feedings a day. Total daily amount based on baby's weight between 28-32 oz in 24 hours
6 months	Breastmilk Formula iron fortified cereal	Feed on demand 6 or more times in 24 hours 4-6 Feeding around 32 oz in 24 hours 1-2 tablespoons, 1-2 times a day
6-9 months	Breastmilk Formula iron fortified cereal Strained vegetables Strained fruits Strained meats plain toast or teething biscuit	3-5 feedings, or as desired by mom and baby 3-5 feedings, 30-33 oz in 24 hours 2-3 tablespoons, 2 times a day 2-3 tablespoons, 2 times a day 2-3 tablespoons, 2 times a day 1-2 tablespoons, 1-2 times a day 1/2 -1 serving
9-12 months	Breastmilk Formula water in a sippy cup iron fortified cereal soft chopped vegetables soft chopped fruits tender chopped meats, avoid hot dogs bread and bread products cottage cheese, plain yogurt, soft cheese	3-4 feedings, or as desired by mom and baby 24-30 oz in 24 hours 3-4 oz 3-4 tablespoons, 2 times a day 3-4 tablespoons, 2 times a day 3-4 tablespoons, 2 times a day 2-3 tablespoons, 2 times a day 1/2-1 serving offer small servings
1 year	Breastmilk whole cows milk, offered in a cup No limit on Solid foods	2-4 feedings or as desired by mom and baby 2-4 feedings 24 oz a day consult pediatrician for new dietary guidelines

Printable version of this chart is available on my website

320

Chapter 21: All Good Things Must Come to an End: Weaning

Every breastfeeding mother comes to a point where she is faced with having to wean her baby. It's often a bittersweet moment. There is joy at being able to eat and drink whatever you want, and go wherever you want...but also sadness, as you may be mourning the loss of those quiet, special moments between you and your baby and that special time of closeness and bonding you shared. Alas, all things come to an end. For some women, this will be an easy decision and for others a hard one. For some it may even be a decision they medically don't have a say in.

Whatever the reason, breastfeeding is an accomplishment you should be proud of, no matter the length of time, whether it was one week or two years. You did a wonderful thing for you and your baby. So now that the time has come, let me walk you through how to dry up your milk supply. The process seems odd, but it works.

I never recommend going cold turkey. Your breasts and your baby won't be happy! I weaned cold turkey and, ladies, let me just say, I had no idea my breasts could hurt so much and turn into the lumpy mountains they became that week. I wanted nothing touching me, not even the warm breeze from outside. It was excruciating.

If you can take a few weeks to wean, do it! Start by replacing one feed a day with a bottle or sippy cup of either expressed breast milk, formula, or cow's milk, if over twelve months. This will allow your cellular breast tissue to gradually realize what's happening and prevent you from becoming severely engorged. Also start gradually shortening the minutes of the other feeds. If you are weaning an older baby, this should not be as difficult. In between feeding and pumping sessions, try not to stimulate your breasts in anyway. It will only make the process last longer.

So let's say you are down to four feeding sessions a day that last no more than five to ten minutes. Begin by bringing each session down to five minutes, then three minutes. Figure out which feed is most important to you and your baby, and then begin with the feed furthest from that time.

Every few days, take a feed away and swap it out with a bottle of pumped milk or formula. If the baby is older, water can also be given. It is important, however, to make sure that the hydration and nutritional needs of the child are met throughout the process, so make sure to monitor the output of diapers. Here is a breakdown of what that would look like:

Week 1	Week 2	Week 3	Week 4
7 a.m. (5–7 min)	7 a.m. (5 min)	7 a.m. (3–5 min)	7 a.m. (3–5 min)

Week 1	Week 2	Week 3	Week 4
12 p.m. (5–7 min)	Skip	Skip	Skip
5 p.m. (5–7 min)	2 p.m. (5 min)	Skip	Skip
10 p.m. (5–7 min)	10 p.m. (5 min)	10 p.m. (5 min)	Skip

After the fourth week, continue to one feed/pump a day until you are ready to stop altogether. The flavor of the milk will become rather bitter, and often your kiddo just stops on her own.

If the gradual weaning process isn't right for you, and you want to quit cold turkey, or medically you need to dry up your supply, then here are the steps to follow:

1. During the drying up stage, it is very important to NOT stimulate your breasts with a pump or massage. This will only make the breasts think they needs to produce more.

2. Buy a head of green cabbage and keep it in the refrigerator to keep it cold and fresh. Peel off the leaves, crush them with a rolling pin to break up the enzymes, then place one leaf on each breast inside a well-fitting bra. (I know that sounds really weird....but cabbage when placed topically secretes enzymes that dry up the production of milk. It works.) Replace the cabbage leaves with fresh ones from the fridge when

323

they become wilted, usually every hour. Be sure to do this for at least twenty-four to forty-eight hours or however long is needed.

3. Wear a tight-fitting bra such as a sports bra that allows you to feel supported but will not cause you to have clogs. Continue taking sunflower lecithin.

4. Use ice packs to bring down the swelling of the breast tissue if you become severely engorged.

5. Peppermint essential oil capsules should be taken both orally and rubbed on the breast tissue. Some whole food stores also sell peppermint oil capsules, but any essential oil from a respected company is the best. Ingest a pellet/capsule every hour. Or you can buy some peppermint Altoids, and eat one Altoids every hour. (You don't have to wear those!) The strong peppermint will lower the milk supply. Peppermint tea works nicely as well.

6. Drinking sage tea or eating parsley salads will also help dry up your milk.

7. Decongestants such as Sudafed or anti-histamines such as Benadryl may be helpful, but this should be done under the care of your physician. Breasts are mucus membranes and will respond to the "drying out" method these drugs produce.

8. Cabo Creme is a wonderful product that works very similarly to the cabbage leaves, hence the name. This

may be a bit easier and you can rub this ointment on as often as you need to.

I do not recommend using any medications designed to stop a woman from lactating, such as Cabergoline. This is often prescribed within the first forty-eight hours after a delivery to prevent milk from coming in, as it is a prolactin inhibitor. I have seen many women try to get this prescribed, but the side effects can be dangerous. The medication is not safe to pass into breastmilk and can drastically lower the mother's blood pressure, causing extreme dizziness.

Eventually your supply will dry up, but the timing will differ from woman to woman. If for some reason these steps are not working, contact a lactation consultant such as myself for further guidance. You may smell like peppermint coleslaw for a few days, but in the end your breasts will be happier that you chose not to just abandon them through this process.

Final Thoughts

Phew! What a journey you have had, my friend. This book has hopefully provided you with some insight and knowledge to ease your concerns when it comes to breastfeeding your little one. This was A LOT of information and might feel a tad overwhelming. I bet you had no idea (much like I didn't) that there could be so many twists and turns to breastfeeding, how cool our bodies could be, and the emotional roller coaster you would go on. Maybe most surprising is how bittersweet it would be to let go of something that you shed literal blood, sweat, and tears over. You will never work harder for something in your life than this, and I can almost guarantee that you will never feel the sense of triumph as you will when you close this chapter of your life.

Mom guilt is real and is caused by the biggest lie you will ever listen too—that you have to be the perfect mom. It is impossible to be the perfect mother. There is no such thing. If you try to be the perfect parent, you are setting yourself up to fail. There are going to be magnificent moments and monumental failures, and both are okay. Even when you feel like you are the absolute worst mom and that you are doing nothing right, I can almost guarantee that your baby is gazing up at you with sweet adoration.

As mothers, we give our all, and when we feel empty, we look at that as failure. If you have to return to work because you are the breadwinner, and that guilt rises up, remind yourself of the beautiful example you are setting for your child. You are modeling strength, endurance, creativity, and self-worth. Being a working mom can be difficult, yes, but it provides an example of endurance. If you are a stay-at-home mom and feel guilty because you aren't out in the world providing, or being the friend or partner you used to be, shut that guilt down, Momma. Being all those things while being a kick-ass mom is demonstrating tenacity.

I wish I could say that one day those moments of guilt will subside, but they are unfortunately par for the course throughout motherhood. Take a moment to seek out the truths within you and around you. You are transforming little hearts and molding a life into a beautiful soul. That takes courage and strength.

As you close the final pages of this guide, I pray that you trust your mom gut with all that you have. Opinions will come and go. Advice will find its way to you. In the end, what matters most is trusting your mom gut. This is YOUR baby! You get to do this YOUR way! Are you going to make mistakes along the way? Oh, absolutely, there is a 100% chance you will. But those mistakes will strengthen you and transform you into a strong momma bear. I am so grateful that I followed my instincts and listened to my child over what any other provider or "expert" told me. My girls are alive today because of instinct. When in doubt, take a moment to pause, reflect, and follow your intuition. It will never fail you.

Every time I end a consult with one of my patients, I sit down next to her, often with her sweet baby in her arms, and we discuss her vision and create a plan to help her reach her goals. I tell them, as I want to tell you, that our relationship doesn't end when you stop breastfeeding. I am here for you. If our goal is to increase duration of breastfeeding, then our charge has to be unity within an ever-changing field. We cannot stop learning. Momma, I implore you to keep learning. To keep seeking. More than anything, take each moment for what it is. The days are long but the years are short. I am so immensely proud of you. Thank you for allowing me to guide you. It truly has been an honor to be your Booby Fairy.

Appendix

What to Look For in a Lactation Consultant

When you have reached difficulty in your breastfeeding journey, finding a skilled IBCLC (Internationally Board Certified Lactation Consultant) can be overwhelming. You are already exhausted, anxious, and simply want to feed your baby. Here is a brief summary of what to look for in a lactation consultant.

1. Make sure they truly are an IBCLC. Many women out there claim to be an IBCLC when in reality they are just certified lactation educators or counselors. The difference is that an IBCLC has had significantly more schooling and is capable of hands-on skilled care. A CLE (Certified Lactation Educator) has only had about three months of training, never took an exam, and is only educated to teach basics on breastfeeding. No hands-on care is provided. You and your baby deserve the real deal.

2. Look at their specialty. Everyone's breastfeeding experience is unique, and some mothers have specific needs that only specialized IBCLCs can treat. I would find out how many years they have been in practice,

whether they have dealt with your concerns in the past, and if they are confident in the skills required.

3. IBCLCs can do hands-on breastfeeding care, hand expression, suck assessments, and breast exams. However, their license does not cover the ability to prescribe any medications, diagnose medical conditions, or perform medical tasks such as needle aspirations unless they are also an MD or other medical professional.

4. Feel them out. You are about to meet with a woman that hopefully connects with your personality. There are IBCLCs with a holistic approach and those with a focus towards Western medicine. It is important that you find a provider that fits your comfort zone and can put you at ease. You are sharing vulnerable information; you should feel safe and comfortable.

5. Price and location. Some IBCLCs are willing to go into the home and do home consults. Some only offer clinic or office hours. Their prices should reflect that. Every IBCLC can set their own price, but I would be leery of anyone who charges by the hour. No mom should feel the pressure of financial burden because of a time constraint. Find out what their fee includes: follow-up care, follow-up visits, texts, calls, emails,

etc... Make sure they have liability insurance and are CPR certified, as well as certified in neonatal resuscitation.

6. Insurance: Most insurance companies will reimburse for lactation care or will allow the IBCLC to bill directly. I would ask if the IBCLC has an established NPI number or tax ID number. Do they offer superbills for insurance coverage?

7. What do their reviews say about them? What have other mommas felt? Look at Yelp, look at their website, and ask your friends. Trust your gut more than anything.

ACKNOWLEDGMENTS

First and foremost I would like to give all glory to God, for without Him, none of this would be possible. When I didn't think I could, this scripture kept me going :Phil 4:13 I CAN do all things through Christ who give me strength!

A BIG thank you to my husband Ryan, who stood by me every step of the way, encouraging me, and providing endless grace and love. You have been my biggest cheerleader

To my incredible daughters Alyssa and Alaina, who without them, I would not have sought out the knowledge and develop the passion I have for mothers and their babies. You girls are my inspiration, my world, and proudest legacy.

To my amazing publicist. Girl, I am so beyond blessed by you, for all you do for my brand, being by my side, and coaching me through this crazy new journey of mine. Without you none of this would be possible.

To Cerina for encouraging me to write this book in the first place, and for providing the inspiring forward to this project. Who would have thought 25 years ago in high school the two of us would be helping mommas all over the world.

To my friends and family, my posse, my BOC, my e-her, my mother, Marguerite, who have walked through life with me, kept me laughing, keep me humble, and encourage me to never give up no matter what. Next cocktail is on me.

To my editor Erica Ellis from Ink-Deep Editing, for the amazing job of organizing my thoughts and putting up with my grammar. Without you this book would be a hot mess.

To my village at Tongue Tie Tribe, Dr. Rosanne Berger, Dr. Michelle Weaver, Katie Byram, SLP. Dr. Melinda Fischer (who also happens to be my badass aunt), April Kurtyak and Lauren Messelbeck, LaC who have taught me, loved me, partnered with me, and were so generous to share their knowledge with me in this book. Together we are changing lives one boob at a time.

To my mentors, Gini Baker, Rose Devigne-Jackiewicz, Sue Jacobson, Anne Faust, Theresa Simko, Joanne DeMarchi who spent countless hours years ago, molding me into the IBCLC I am today.

Finally to the many mothers and babies who have given me the honor of walking along side you, learning from you, and inspiring me to be the best IBCLC I can be. You are strong, fierce mommas. Each and every one of you have left an imprint in my heart, and I am beyond blessed by your stories and strength.

INDEX

335

337

341

ENDNOTES

[1] Lori Feldman-Winter and Jay Goldsmith, "Safe Sleep and Skin-to-Skin Care in the Neonatal Period for Healthy Term Newborns," *Pediatrics* (2016): 138(3): e20161889, https://publications.aap.org/pediatrics/article/138/3/e20161889/52741/Safe-Sleep-and-Skin-to-Skin-Care-in-the-Neonatal.

[2] Elizabeth R. Moore, RNC, PhD, IBCLC and Gene Cranston Anderson RN, PhD, "Randomized Controlled Trial of Very Early Mother-Infant Skin-to-Skin Contact and Breastfeeding Status," *Journal of Midwifery and Women's Health* (March-April, 2007): 52(2): 116-125.

[3] Marsha Walker, *Breastfeeding Management for the Clinician, 4th edition* (Burlington, MA: Jones & Bartlett Learning, 2017), 672.

[4] Cincinnati Children's Hospital Medical Center, "Why some women don't have enough breastmilk for baby: Important role of insulin in making breast milk identified," *ScienceDaily* (July 5, 2013): https://www.sciencedaily.com/releases/2013/07/130705212228.htm.

[5] Linda J Kvist, Marie Louise Hall-Lord, Hakan Rydhstroem, and Bodil Wilde Larsson, "A randomised-controlled trial in Sweden of acupuncture and care interventions for the relief of inflammatory symptoms of the breast during lactation," *Midwifery* (June, 2007): 23(2):184-95.

[6] Ping Lu, MSa; Zhi-qi Ye, MSb; Jin Qiu, PhDc; Xiao-yu Wang, MSd; Juan-juan Zheng, PhDa, "Acupoint-tuina therapy promotes lactation in postpartum women with insufficient milk production who underwent caesarean sections," *Medicine* (August, 2019): 98(35): e16456.

[7] Healthcare Medicine Institute, "Acupuncture Boosts Breast Milk Production," https://www.healthcmi.com/Acupuncture-Continuing-Education-News/1773-acupuncture-boosts-breast-milk-production (accessed February, 2022).

[8] Hong-Cai Wang 1, Jun-Ming An, Ying Han, Lin-Na Huang, Jing-Wen Zhao, Li-Xin Wei, Lan Dong, Gui-Rong Zhai, Xiu-Ping Li, Ai-Jun Yang, and Mei Gu, "Multicentral randomized controlled studies on acupuncture at Shaoze (SI 1) for treatment of postpartum hypolactation," Zhongguo Zhen Jiu (February, 2007): 27(2):85-8.

[9] National Center for Biotechnology Information, "Domperidone," https://www.ncbi.nlm.nih.gov/books/NBK501371/ (accessed February, 2022).

[10] University of Rochester Medical Center, "Can Mother's Milk Help Fight COVID? New Evidence Suggests Yes," https://www.urmc.rochester.edu/news/story/can-mothers-milk-help-fight-covid (accessed February, 2022).

[11] Thomas W. Hale, PhD, *Hale's Medications & Mothers' Milk 2021: A Manual of Lactational Pharmacology – An Essential Reference Manual on the Transmission of Medicine into Breast Milk, 19th Edition* (New York: Springer Publishing Company, 2021), 235

[12] Thomas W. Hale, PhD, *Hale's Medications & Mothers' Milk 2021: A Manual of Lactational Pharmacology – An Essential Reference Manual on the Transmission of Medicine into Breast Milk, 19th Edition* (New York: Springer Publishing Company, 2021), 235

[13] National Center for Biotechnology Information, "Cannabis," https://www.ncbi.nlm.nih.gov/books/NBK501587/ (accessed February, 2022)

[14] National Center for Biotechnology Information, "Cannabis" https://www.ncbi.nlm.nih.gov/pmc/articles/PMC6317767/(accessed February, 2022

[15] National Center for Biotechnology Information, "Nicotine," https://www.ncbi.nlm.nih.gov/books/NBK501586 (accessed February, 2022).

[16] Bridget E. Young, PhD; Antti E. Seppo, PhD; Nichole Diaz, BA; et al, "Association of Human Milk Antibody Induction, Persistence, and Neutralizing Capacity With SARS-CoV-2 Infection vs mRNA Vaccination," *JAMA Pediatrics* (2022): 176(2): 159-168.

343

Made in the USA
Monee, IL
30 September 2024

66840313R00193